My Pantry

MY PANTRY

Alice Waters

with
Fanny Singer

ILLUSTRATIONS BY FANNY SINGER

PAM KRAUSS BOOKS

NEW YORK

ALSO FROM ALICE WATERS AND CHEZ PANISSE

The Art of Simple Food II
40 Years of Chez Panisse: The Power of Gathering
The Art of Simple Food
In the Green Kitchen
Chez Panisse Fruit
Chez Panisse Café Cookbook
Chez Panisse Vegetables
Fanny at Chez Panisse
Chez Panisse Cooking
Chez Panisse Desserts
Chez Panisse Pasta, Pizza, and Calzone
Chez Panisse Menu Cookbook

Copyright © 2015 by Alice Waters. Illustrations copyright © 2015 by Fanny Singer. All rights reserved. Published in the United States by Pam Krauss Books, an imprint of the Crown Publishing Group, a division of Penguin Random House LLC, New York. www.crownpublishing.com.

PAM KRAUSS BOOKS and colophon are trademarks of Penguin Random House LLC.

Library of Congress Cataloging-in-Publication Data
Waters, Alice, author.
My pantry / Alice Waters ; illustrations by Fanny Singer.—First edition.
pages cm. Includes index.
1. Cooking, French. 2. Spices. I. Singer, Fanny, 1983– illustrator. II. Title.
TX719.W3425 2015
641.5944—dc23   2014042977

ISBN 978-0-8041-8528-8
Ebook ISBN 978-0-8041-8529-5

Printed in the United States of America

10 9 8 7 6 5 4 3 2 1

First Edition

To Samantha Greenwood,
dear friend and indispensable collaborator

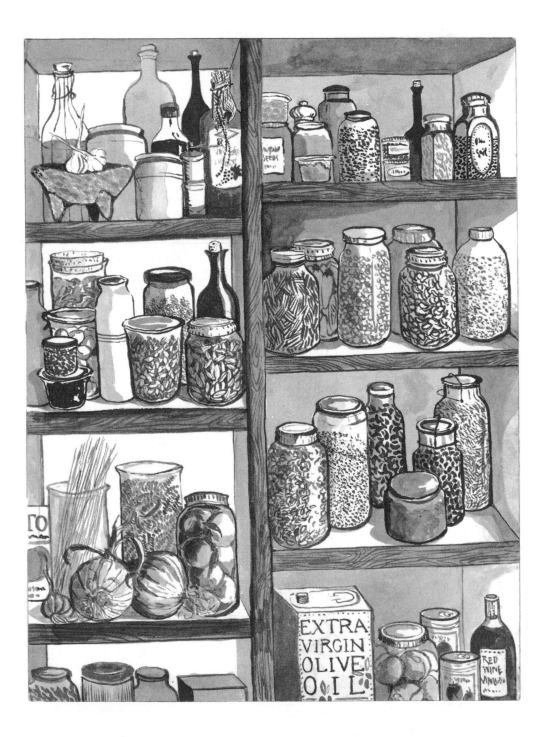

CONTENTS

7. Cheese

8. Sweet Preserves

Books
Acknowledgments
Index

Introduction

When I come back home from a trip, one of the first things I need to do is walk into my kitchen and look around. It always makes me feel better when I know exactly where I am. First I see, next to the stove, the old Middle Eastern copper tray, and on it the glass cruet of vinegar, and the pepper mill and friendly little bowls of salt mixtures and chile flakes; and I open the cupboard, and spot the pasta and lentils and beans, and look up and see a beautiful row of jars of homemade preserved tomatoes alternating with jars of apricots sparkling in syrup. There's the crock of chestnut honey, where it belongs; there're the tin boxes filled with cumin and coriander seeds, if I want to toast and grind a spoonful or two. And I feel flooded with relief and comforted by the knowledge that, no matter how tired I am, at least I'll be able to dream up something to cook—something delicious!—and right away, too. In maybe five minutes I can have some pasta on the stove: I have that preserved tomato, there are herbs (I always think of my herb garden as a living extension of my pantry), there may even be a wedge of grating cheese. A familiar pantry is like being surrounded by friends who won't let you down, within instant reach.

Simplicity and economy and ease in the kitchen all come from having a pantry you've made your own from ingredients you've mixed and made yourself. Such a pantry is not just a shortcut to cooking something special in a hurry (a jar of caponata, say, for an instant delicious pasta sauce); it also encourages the best kind of impromptu cooking. A well-stocked pantry helps you think creatively about how to feed yourself, and anyone who happens to be with you, a thoughtfully prepared, flavorful, and wholesome meal, without expending very much time or effort. I've come to realize that it's the way I use my pantry, more than any individual ingredient, recipe, or technique, that defines my personal cooking aesthetic. And my pantry contains not just the staples you would expect, but the extra seasonings, condiments, and embellishments—for lack of a better term, the grace notes—that truly define my cooking and my home.

My pantry is always changing. I get exposed to flavors I've never tasted before, and my pantry has to adjust. For example, when I first visited Italy many years ago, I tasted ingredients that were completely new to me then that have since become absolute essentials. The flavors of green-gold Tuscan olive oil, syrupy aged balsamic vinegar, sun-dried tomatoes, chestnut honey, and fresh, grassy buffalo mozzarella really woke me up; I wanted to fill a suitcase and smuggle all these things back with me to the United States (in fact I *did* smuggle back more than a few!). Little by little, with the encouragement of hungry cooks like myself, farmers and artisanal producers throughout California and beyond began making similar products: delicious fruity olive oil, tangy fresh goat cheese, caramel-y wildflower honey, and exquisite sun-blushed tomatoes. I'm somewhat ashamed to admit, though, that it was only fairly recently I realized some of these things could easily be made at home. With a memory of ricotta made from the milk of sheep pastured in the Roman Campagna in my mind, I began experimenting with making my own cheeses. Many of the other flavors and ingredients I once considered rarefied and unobtainable, I now make in my own kitchen. And as global connectivity increases, it's easier to find such things as sumac and Marash chile peppers. In short, it's an exciting time for the pantry!

So here is my advice, and a few handfuls of recipes, for making some beautiful and delicious things with ingredients that can easily be in anyone's kitchen. Just remember, sometimes the best dishes are the simplest:

a drizzle of warmed honey over a slice of fresh ricotta, or the "Coming Home Pasta" I always make for myself when I return from a trip: spaghetti tossed with a heap of sautéed garlic, dried chile flakes, the odd salted anchovy, and a handful of chopped parsley. And remember, too, that sometimes the greatest, most complex effects are produced by the smallest causes: A pinch of saffron, for example, can be magic.

Organizing your pantry is not just a practical approach to cooking; it will help you economize and minimize your environmental impact, too. You can make your kitchen a lot greener by making some ingredients yourself instead of buying them readymade. Consider, for example, the difference in waste and carbon expense—not to mention the difference in cost—when you make your own yogurt in reusable glass jars instead of driving to a store to buy it in disposable plastic containers. Plus, when you make something yourself, you always know exactly what's in it and you can be sure about the healthfulness of your food. And perhaps most important of all, making your own allows you to experiment with a recipe and adjust it according to your own palate.

Some simple things in this book I prepare and keep on hand routinely, but many other preparations I make only now and then, depending on a host of factors: whether I happen to visit a friend who is sharing a bumper crop of backyard berries this summer, for example, or whether this is the year I feel a compulsion to confit every Early Girl tomato in sight, so that I can be sure to have enough to see me through the winter. My pantry is always changing, gradually, along with my taste, from season to season and from year to year: This evolution is what makes it distinctively mine. My hope is that this book will inspire you to make your pantry distinctively *yours*.

⋇

CHAPTER ONE

SPICE MIXTURES

and

CONDIMENTS

Perhaps the most coveted real estate in my kitchen, the spot right next to my stove, is occupied by my spice tray, an old copper tray with a deep patina, which I picked up long ago, in Turkey, I think. This tray is home to a carafe of homemade vinegar surrounded by at least half a dozen little ceramic and wooden bowls containing various salts and salt mixtures and spices and different kinds of dried chiles. While I keep a number of other seasonings in a nearby drawer, these few select ingredients are so indispensable to my cooking that I won't have them anywhere other than stoveside, where they're within reach. Different seasonings can take the same dish in quite different directions: a pinch of cumin on roasted squash, for example, might suggest India, while a dusting of fennel pollen might call to mind the late-summer hills of California. Fresh herbs, of course, can be counted on to achieve similar shifts in flavor, but spices and chiles can be used year-round to explore new, less familiar territory.

The chile peppers have particularly captured my attention lately. I constantly find myself buying different types on my travels and I always relish the gift of a new kind of chile from a friend. Of course, there are thousands of varieties, and spiciness can vary drastically—even among peppers of the same variety. Just as some jalapeños are searingly hot and others are as sweet as bell peppers, some dried chiles might blister the palate where others mostly add sweetness. For this reason, it's incredibly important to taste your chile powders and flakes before adding any quantity to a dish. The chile peppers I prefer—Marash, Espelette, sweet paprika, and smoked pasilla—all add more flavor (smokiness, sweetness, depth . . .) than heat.

It is relatively easy to come by dried chiles, but it's also easy to dry your own, using either fresh ones you've bought at the store or farmers' market or ones you've grown and harvested yourself. Grinding home-dried chiles, making your own chile powders, and creating simple spice mixes will open up your cooking to new dimensions and flavors, and also allow you to taste and adjust the ingredients in your spice mixtures as you like them. And you can make as much as you want or need at a time. Some of the spice mixtures you'll want to make in small quantities; for example, once you've toasted and ground up seeds such as cumin and sesame, they rapidly lose their aromatic intensity. In general, I recommend buying spices in small amounts—this way you'll avoid the problem of stale spices that lack the pungency and flavor of truly fresh ones. Of course, the very best way to ensure your spices are fresh is to go to the source; everyone who can keep a garden should let a few plants go to seed. For example, if you grow cilantro, plant enough to let some go to flower so that you can collect and dry the coriander seeds. The same goes for fennel, which will not only sprout into beautiful golden-crowned stalks, it will yield one of the most ambrosial of spices: fennel pollen, a delight to use in cooking and a beloved food of the bees!

Za'atar

It was only quite recently that I began to make and use this sesame spice mix at home. I love the savory edge it lends when sprinkled over crostini, or salads, or my go-to breakfast of whole-wheat flatbread spread with hummus. This za'atar recipe was shared with me by my friend Suzanne Drexhage, the owner of Bartavelle in Berkeley. She offers this blend with her Persian breakfast, a combination of cheese and yogurt served with fresh herbs and pickles. I also like to dust it generously over poached eggs.

Mix together one part sumac, one part dried thyme, and one part white sesame seeds. Measure this quantity and add an equal amount of Maldon salt (or another flaky sea salt). Stir to combine and store in a tightly covered jar.

Cumin Salt

MAKES ABOUT 2 TABLESPOONS

Cumin is one of the spices I use most; it is much more versatile than people imagine. I use it so often, in fact, that it is always among the flavorings on the spice tray I keep next to my stove. I add it to sautéed greens and lentils, and I use it to season halved hard-boiled eggs for a quick savory breakfast. When my daughter was little I sometimes strewed a touch of cumin salt over carrot sticks to put in her lunchbox. She loved it!

2 tablespoons cumin seeds   *1 teaspoon sea salt*

Heat a small sauté pan or skillet over medium heat. Add the cumin seeds and toast them until they are just beginning to color. Use a mortar and pestle to pound the toasted seeds and salt together until coarsely ground.

Chile-Lime Salt

MAKES ABOUT 2 TABLESPOONS

I serve a small bowl of chile-lime salt with platters of radishes and carrots. It's also delicious dusted over cold mango or watermelon wedges in the height of summer, or over a section of orange as an accompaniment to a glass of mescal.

1 tablespoon sea salt
1 tablespoon spicy ground
chile

Zest of 1 lime, finely zested
with a very sharp grater

Stir together the salt, chile, and lime zest. Stored in a tightly covered container, this will keep for several months.

Niloufer's Masala

Besides being one of my oldest and dearest friends, Niloufer Ichaporia King is one of the great cooks. Every spring when she takes the reins in the Chez Panisse kitchen and cooks a Parsi New Year's feast, the restaurant is flooded with the intoxicating perfume of her spice arsenal. I find myself yearning for Parsi New Year all year long, which is why I like to keep Niloufer's masala on hand to add a bit of her culinary flair to whatever I'm cooking. I use it as a dry rub for fish, shellfish, chicken, or lamb; stir it into yogurt; and sprinkle it on scrambled eggs.

Mix together equal parts cayenne pepper, ground turmeric, and fine sea salt. Start with a tablespoon of each. If you find you are using it often, you can make it in bigger batches if you want; it will keep for months in a covered container stored somewhere cool and dry.

Nico's Pork Seasoning

This is a two-part seasoning for pork and other meat inspired by the garlicky herb sauce and multipurpose dry spice mix that my godson Nico Monday uses at his restaurants in Gloucester, Massachusetts, Short & Main and The Market. This combination of spices reminds me of Italy, of the sweet and spicy notes that flavor so many of my favorite dishes there. When I use it for pork chops, porchetta, or a simple roast chicken, I like to slather the garlicky herb sauce on the meat before cooking and then sprinkle on the dried spice mixture. The combination of fennel pollen and Marash pepper bleeds into the meat giving it a beautiful rusty saffron color. Though it was originally intended as a seasoning for meat, lately I've found myself tossing roasted vegetables and sautéed greens with it. The fennel adds a wonderful sweetness.

For the garlicky herb slather: Pound together in a mortar and pestle (preferably one with a 3- to 4-cup bowl) garlic (or green garlic, if available), sage leaves, rosemary, coarse salt, and a small amount of olive oil. Rub this generously all over the meat. Set aside.

For the dry spices: Start with a clean, dry mortar and pestle. Measure equal parts fennel seeds, cumin seeds, coriander seeds, fennel pollen, and Marash pepper. Combine the fennel seed, cumin, and coriander seeds in the mortar and grind until pulverized. Add the same quantity of fennel pollen and Marash pepper and stir together. Sprinkle over the meat and roast or grill.

Espelette Hot Sauce

MAKES ABOUT ½ CUP

Because Espelette chiles are intensely flavorful without being over-whelmingly spicy, I use this easy-to-make hot sauce all the time. Its balance of sweetness and heat tempered with Champagne vinegar makes an especially good complement to garden salad tacos, one of my lunch staples. It's also wonderful drizzled over egg dishes or stirred into a bowl of warm beans and greens.

½ cup Champagne vinegar
2 tablespoons Espelette chile
    powder

1½ teaspoons sea salt

Combine all the ingredients in a blender and purée for 30 seconds. Pour into a small jar, cover, and refrigerate for up to 3 months.

Red Wine Vinegar

I've been making my own red wine vinegar for the past thirty years. While this may sound a bit advanced or arcane, I promise you it is not: Making vinegar is easy, it tastes delicious, and it's a great way to make use of unfinished half- or quarter-bottles of wine. It just takes time.

To begin all you need is a vinegar starter culture—called a "mother"— much as you use a starter to make sourdough bread or yogurt. (The "mother" is the foggy substance that floats suspended in vinegar; the beneficial bacteria in this little cloud are responsible for converting the alcohol into acid.) If you have any friends who are already making vinegar, you can just take a little of their vinegar mother to get the ball rolling—I got mine in the early 1980s from my friend the food writer Richard Olney, and it has such sentimental value it practically feels like a member of the family. Vinegar mothers can be purchased at winemaking supply stores, but you'd do just as well to use one from any good bottle of unpasteurized vinegar from the farmers' market.

Once a year, I fill a 10-liter oak barrel (you can get this online or at a winemaking supply store) with the vinegar mother and all the unfin- ished bottles of wine that I've accumulated over the past six months—a lot of red, but also rosé, white, sparkling, whatever I have. (As the wine accumulates, I decant it into a few bottles and cork them tightly until I'm ready to begin the vinegar process.) Most people won't need quite so large a barrel, but I use a lot of vinegar—I have a salad every day!—and I like to give some away to friends. I use oak because it gives the vinegar a unique depth, but if you can't find an oak barrel, there's also the option of using a ceramic pot or jug. The container should have an opening at the top (which you cover with cheesecloth) so that the vinegar can breathe.

Then I leave it—for a year, ideally, because I like that aged, oaky flavor that comes with time. The longer you leave it in that oak, the better and mellower it gets. When the year is up, I transfer most of it to a glass jug with a spigot, then taste and adjust. I love this part—tweaking and adjusting to get it just how I like it. When I taste my vinegar and it isn't quite right (if it's too acidic, for example), I'll add something a little sweeter to it, like a Spanish sherry vinegar, or a few drops of balsamic. You can also use a little water to adjust it—or cider vinegar if you like that apple taste. Then I decant the finished vinegar into a smaller container to keep next to the olive oil, salt, and pepper, and refill it whenever I run out. Wine vinegar has so many uses: Beyond the vinaigrettes I make every day, I use it in marinades and sauces, or splash a little over some garlicky sautéed greens to brighten the flavors.

If you want to learn more about vinegar-making, Richard Olney's classic book *Simple French Food* has a wonderful, in-depth explanation, and Sandor Katz's *The Art of Fermentation* is also a thorough resource. Perhaps the most important thing to remember is that you should always add wine that you actually like to drink—bad wine makes bad vinegar!

Apple Peel Cider Vinegar

MAKES 1¾ QUARTS

The leftover cores and peels of apples can be transformed into a wonderful vinegar. Rather than throwing away the scraps after you make a pie or tart, freeze them, and when you have enough, make this mellow, fruity vinegar.

2 quarts apple cores and peels   2 quarts water

⅓ cup sugar

Put the apple cores and peels in a large glass or ceramic bowl. Dissolve the sugar in the water and pour over the cores and peels. Cover with a plate and weight down with something heavy to keep the solids submerged. Cover the entire bowl with cheesecloth or a kitchen towel and leave on the counter out of direct sunlight for 7 days.

Strain the cores and peels from the liquid and discard the solids. Put the liquid in jars or bottles and secure a piece of cheesecloth over the opening with a rubber band to allow airflow. Allow to age at room temperature out of direct sunlight for 6 to 8 weeks, until the desired flavor is achieved. A "mother" will begin to develop after about 2 weeks.

NOTE

~ This vinegar is delicious with sparkling water, as a soda or "shrub." Start with equal parts vinegar and sparkling water and adjust to taste.

Tahini

MAKES ABOUT 1½ CUPS

While homemade tahini is never quite as smooth as store-bought, the exceptionally nutty and fresh flavor is so much better. I add tahini to so many dishes, from chickpeas to yogurt; or use it as a salad dressing with a little garlic, olive oil, and lemon juice. I also like to spread it on Whole-Wheat Flatbreads (page 79), adding a dusting of ground red chile for a savory breakfast or a drizzle of honey for a sweet one.

2 cups hulled sesame seeds

2 to 4 tablespoons extra-virgin olive oil

¼ teaspoon sea salt

Lightly toast the sesame seeds in a skillet over medium heat, stirring frequently to ensure they don't burn. They are sufficiently toasted when their aroma is released and just a few are turning golden brown, about 2 minutes. Immediately transfer to a food processor to cool.

Purée the sesame seeds for a couple of minutes until they form a granular paste. Add 2 tablespoons of the oil and the salt and purée 1 to 2 minutes more, stopping to scrape down the sides with a rubber spatula if necessary. The paste will eventually soften and become more fluid. If this isn't happening, add more oil, a tablespoon at a time, puréeing for another minute after each addition.

Store in an airtight jar in the refrigerator for up to 1 month.

CHAPTER TWO

NUTS

There's nothing quite like roasting almonds or walnuts for creating atmosphere; they instantly invoke the sense that the kitchen is being cooked in, and give the room a wonderful, slightly caramel smell. Whenever I'm feeling hungry for a little bite of something savory, or when I know friends are coming for dinner, I like to make a batch of roasted nuts tossed with herbs and sea salt. Guests instantly gravitate toward that plate: Perfectly toasted nuts are irresistible. Likewise, there's hardly a better way to end a meal than with a plate of nut-packed dark chocolate bark, candied citrus peel, and dates stuffed with almond paste. It's their sheer versatility that makes nuts such an indispensable ingredient in my pantry. They can be used in hundreds of ways and are equally delicious in all kinds of savory and sweet preparations—not to mention, they are incredibly good for you.

The last few years, I've watched with concern as the almond-growing industry in California has come under considerable strain, both because of the severity of the ongoing drought and because a crisis is facing the bees that pollinate the orchards. While no one knows precisely what has caused the recent bee colony collapse, I'm not alone in believing that the monoculture of the commercial almond industry has left these essential pollinators vulnerable.

Without the bees, we wouldn't have any almonds—or squash, most berries, onions, kiwis, avocados, quince, or lemons to name just a few of the many bee-dependent crops. This is why I try to make a point of buying only organic almonds, usually from the farmers' market, so I know that the nuts I'm buying aren't having a negative impact on the land, or the live ecosystem that keeps it healthy and productive. Buying almonds from a local producer also means keeping in step with seasonality and freshness.

This is especially important because almonds are so perishable. Because of their high content of healthy oils, nuts tend to go rancid very quickly—especially walnuts, pecans, pine nuts, and pistachios. This is why I recommend buying nuts in the fall when they are at their seasonal peak, and keeping them in airtight containers for near-immediate use. Nuts stay fresher longer if stored in the refrigerator, but rather than storing large quantities of nuts at home, I favor buying small amounts often from the farmers who harvested them because they are likely to have been well stored.

I've recently started making fresh nut milk. Almond is my favorite variety of nut to use for this purpose; it yields a creamy, fragrant milk that reminds me of the quivering blancmange that Richard Olney used to serve with a glass of Sauternes on hot Provençal evenings. Sometimes when we make almond desserts like blancmange at Chez Panisse we add *noyaux*, the kernels inside the pits of stone fruits, to deepen the flavor. The kernels look and taste like small almonds but are generally more fragrant and a bit more bitter. The kind we use most frequently comes from the stones of apricots. Noyau ice cream has been an enduring and beloved fixture of the Chez Panisse dessert repertoire, but noyaux are also wonderful in apricot jam or roasted and salted and sprinkled over salads.

The recipes in this chapter represent just a fraction of the many uses of all the kinds of nuts that are readily available. And even within each nut family, different varietals will be available depending on where you live. Wherever you are, look for a local farmer with nut trees. And experiment! Try other nuts or seeds in your nut milk. Add spices like curry powder to your roasted nuts instead of herbs. Add roasted nuts to salads and grains to lend richness.

Slow-Roasted Nuts with Sage Leaves

MAKES ABOUT 3½ CUPS

Roasting a mixture of nuts at a low temperature is a wonderful method. At high temperatures, some kinds of nuts in the mixture may burn, but they won't if roasted with the others at a low temperature. The delightfully crisped sage leaves are as satisfying as the roasted nuts themselves.

1 cup walnuts

1 cup almonds

1 cup pecans

1½ cups loosely packed sage leaves

3 tablespoons extra-virgin olive oil

1 teaspoon sea salt

Preheat the oven to 275°F. Line a rimmed baking sheet with parchment paper.

In a medium bowl, mix together the nuts and sage leaves. Add the oil and salt and toss gently until the nuts and sage are evenly coated.

Spread the nuts and sage on the baking sheet and bake for 20 minutes. Stir the nuts and return them to the oven for 10 more minutes. Remove the pan from the oven and break a few nuts open. If their centers are golden brown they are done; if the nuts still need more time, stir them and return them to the oven, checking every 5 minutes or so. You want them to roast fully, not burn. I usually find 35 minutes is about right.

Almond Paste

MAKES ABOUT 1¾ CUPS (ABOUT 14 OUNCES)

This almond paste uses a little less sugar than conventional recipes, allowing the almond flavor to come through more strongly. It's wonderful in cookie and cake recipes that call for almond paste, and can stand on its own rolled into little candies or stuffed into dates.

2 cups raw organic almonds
1 cup organic powdered sugar
¼ cup egg whites (about 2)

1 teaspoon almond extract or Noyau Extract (page 32)
¼ teaspoon salt

Bring a pot of water to a boil and add the almonds. After 30 seconds, drain and rinse with cold water. The skins will have loosened and will easily slip off. Remove the skins and spread the blanched, skinless almonds on a clean kitchen towel to dry completely.

Once dry, grind the almonds in a food processor until fine. Add the sugar, egg whites, almond extract, and salt. Purée until smooth—a couple minutes more. Store in an airtight container in the refrigerator for a month or two, or longer in the freezer.

VARIATIONS

᠖ Add grated lemon or orange zest to the almond paste and use it to stuff dates. Garnish with a few slivered, lightly toasted pistachios.

᠖ Add 3 tablespoons of fine ground coffee and 2 teaspoons Cognac to the almond paste. Roll into balls and roll the balls in granulated sugar to coat them.

Noyau Extract

MAKES ABOUT 1 CUP

Noyaux are the kernels of stone fruit, and their heady bitter-almond aroma infuses sweets like amaretti and liqueurs like amaretto. Like bitter almonds and apple seeds, raw noyaux contain a poisonous cyanide compound, which fortunately can be destroyed by heat. Nonetheless they retain a rather exotic, dangerous reputation that may enhance their appeal for some!

I like to make noyau extract as an alternative to store-bought almond extract. Noyau extract can be added to almond paste and used in any recipe that calls for almond extract. It naturally complements and enhances the flavor of any dessert made with nectarines, plums, cherries, apricots, or peaches.

To obtain enough pits to make extract, I save them over the summer months and when I have enough, I make extract for the coming year. Noyau extract makes a wonderful gift, so I make the largest batch I can.

1 cup apricot pits   *1 cup good-quality vodka*

Preheat the oven to 350°F.

Spread the apricot pits on a rimmed baking sheet and bake for 10 to 15 minutes. Let cool for a couple of minutes. (Leave the oven on.) When the pits are cool enough to handle, put in a clean kitchen towel and use a hammer to gently break the pits open, one by one. Don't hit the pit too hard; it will be easier to remove the kernel from the pit if it is intact.

When all of the soft inner kernels are extracted, return them to the oven and roast them for 5 minutes more. Allow them to cool again. Put the kernels (you should have about ¼ cup) and the vodka in a blender and purée until the kernels are finely ground.

Transfer the purée to a jar, cover tightly, and set in a cool place. Give the jar a shake every day or so. After 10 days, strain the liquid through a fine-mesh sieve into the jar and close with a lid. The extract can be stored indefinitely at room temperature.

Almond Milk

MAKES ABOUT 4 CUPS

The taste of homemade almond milk is ethereal and nothing like pasteurized commercial brands, which often contain preservatives and thickening agents. I use almond milk on porridge or granola in the morning, and as a refreshing drink any time.

1 cup raw organic almonds, soaked in water overnight in the refrigerator

A pinch of sea salt (optional)

Drain the almonds and combine them in a blender with 4 cups water and the salt (if using). Purée until the almonds are completely pulverized. Reserving the pulp, strain the almond milk into a pitcher through a very fine-mesh sieve or a double layer of cheesecloth.

Return the pulp to the blender, add 1 cup water, and blend once more until the almond and water are well mixed, 30 seconds to 1 minute. Strain into the same pitcher and mix with the first batch of almond milk.

Pour into jars, cover, and store in the refrigerator for up to 4 days. The milk will separate when refrigerated and will need to be lightly shaken before using.

VARIATIONS
- To sweeten, purée 1 date with the strained almond milk.
- For a refreshing drink, add a cardamom pod, 1 date, and ⅛ to ¼ teaspoon rose water to the blender when puréeing the pulp the second time. Serve chilled or over ice.

◡ For almond-coconut milk, substitute ½ cup shredded coconut for ½ cup of almonds. Soak the coconut overnight with the almonds and proceed as above.

◡ At the height of summer, purée fresh peaches and figs with almond milk and serve over ice.

◡ Make hazelnut milk instead of almond milk by replacing the almonds with hazelnuts, soaking and puréeing them just as you would the almonds.

◡ For an even creamier milk, replace one-third of the almonds with cashews. The benign flavor of cashews won't interfere with the almond taste, but their higher fat content will yield a richer milk.

Chocolate Nut Bark

MAKES ABOUT A 9 × 11-INCH RECTANGLE

Chocolate nut bark makes a beautiful handmade gift and is a perfect small dessert to have on hand for unexpected guests. I vary the nuts sometimes, but I always seem to come back to a combination of hazelnuts, pistachios, and almonds. Sometimes I also throw in some chopped dried sour cherries to add a fruity, tangy dimension. This recipe is not complicated, but you will need to temper the chocolate, a process of heating and cooling that gives the final product a glossy sheen and smooth texture. The tempering process is not superfluous. When melted chocolate has the proper molecular structure, it solidifies with a shiny surface and will break into pieces cleanly. This method of tempering was inspired by the example of Alice Medrich, a great chocolatier in Berkeley, who adds chunks of chocolate to hot, melted chocolate to slow the melting process and build the proper molecular structure.

Butter or neutral vegetable oil, for the pan

12 ounces good-quality bittersweet chocolate, 65 to 70% cacao

1½ cups chopped or sliced toasted nuts

Have ready an instant-read thermometer, a heatproof spatula, a plate, and a butter knife. Line a rimmed baking sheet with parchment paper and coat a 9 × 11-inch section of the paper with butter or oil.

If the chocolate is in large blocks, chop it into ¼-inch chunks and set aside 4 ounces. Sift the chopped nuts in a coarse-mesh sieve to remove any loose skins.

Heat a few inches of water in a saucepan until barely simmering. Put 8 ounces of the chocolate in a heatproof bowl and set over the water.

(The water should not touch the bowl.) As the chocolate begins to melt, stir constantly until it is about 75 percent melted. At this point, check the temperature with the instant-read thermometer. If the temperature exceeds 100°F, remove the bowl from the heat and let the chocolate cool, continuing to stir. When the temperature reaches 100°F, add the reserved 4 ounces of chocolate and continue to stir over the simmering water until all of the chocolate is melted. Check the temperature again, and once the chocolate has reached 90°F, turn off the heat and test to see if it has tempered properly by drizzling a little chocolate onto the blade of the butter knife and setting it aside on the plate in a cool place. Continue stirring the chocolate for 3 minutes, then check to see if the chocolate on the butter knife has hardened. If it has, it is tempered. If it hasn't, test again; the chocolate will have cooled a little more and it usually tempers perfectly the second time.

Add half the nuts (¾ cup) to the chocolate and stir to combine. Pour the mixture onto the prepared section of the parchment paper, using the spatula to spread it to a rectangular shape about 7 × 9 inches. Evenly sprinkle the remaining nuts on top.

Set in a cool place to harden. I like to leave the nut bark in a large block for storing in an airtight container and then break off pieces to serve on a dessert plate. Use within 1 month for best flavor.

VARIATIONS

᠃ Vary the combination of nuts or add chopped dried sour cherries to the mix, decreasing the nuts proportionately.
᠃ Add ¼ cup chopped candied citrus zest to the nut mixture, decreasing the nuts by ¼ cup.
᠃ Scrape the melted chocolate (without nuts) into a pastry bag and pipe out individual candies. Top with toasted pistachios or hazelnuts and sour cherries. It helps to have a second person on hand to do this job, as the chocolate may harden before you have a chance to top it!

CHAPTER THREE

BEANS

and

OTHER LEGUMES

When it comes to foods that are wholesome, economical, filling, and delicious, nothing rivals the legume family. Beans, lentils, lupines, peas, and peanuts all belong to a subclass of legumes called grain legumes, or pulses. Legumes are one of the best sources of vegetable protein there is and almost every culture has its own beloved version of a bean and grain dish, whether it's Indian lentil dal with rice, Mexican beans and corn tortillas, Italian pasta e fagioli, or Middle Eastern hummus and pita bread.

Beans can make a simple tasty meal on their own or be an element of a larger whole. Especially in the autumn and winter, I often cook a big pot of beans to use throughout the week. Sometimes I cook them with a mirepoix (finely minced and sautéed onion, celery, and carrot) and sometimes I just add a halved onion while they're cooking (which I fish out when the beans are tender). Like brown rice, cooked beans keep well for a few days in the refrigerator and can be used as the basis for quick and pleasing meals. As with so many ingredients, the simplest preparation is often the most satisfying—there are few things I enjoy more than a hot bowl of beans with a sprinkle of sea salt and a generous drizzle of fruity extra-virgin olive oil.

My favorite way to prepare beans is in the fireplace. If you have a fireplace, try it yourself: You will love the smoky flavor that infuses the beans. Even if you don't have a hearth at the ready, though, beans cooked on the stovetop are just as delicious and versatile. Add fully cooked beans to vegetable soups to give them more body and flavor (not to mention protein and fiber); make quick bean tacos with lightly toasted fresh corn tortillas; spoon beans over warm brown rice or alongside sautéed greens for a quick, wholesome lunch.

Lentils, another member of the legume family, are just as versatile as beans and cook much more quickly (and don't require soaking in advance). A pot of lentils prepared at the start of the week can be used cold in salads, warmed in a skillet with a mirepoix as an accompaniment to braised or grilled meat, or added to a fragrant chicken stock to make a simple, satisfying soup.

Chickpeas—in the form of hummus—have meanwhile become an indispensable part of my diet. Many mornings my breakfast will consist of a whole-wheat flatbread toasted over an open flame spread with a spoonful of homemade hummus and a dusting of Marash pepper. I've become so fanatical about making hummus—especially laced with chopped-up bits of preserved lemons—that hardly a week passes without my making a fresh bowl to have in the fridge. It also makes a wonderful afternoon snack: Spoon some into a bowl and arrange some colorful and crunchy vegetables around it. Children and adults alike just love it.

One thing I cannot emphasize enough is the importance of buying fresh dried beans. Unfortunately, many of the beans in markets have been sitting there for some time. Stale beans are salvageable; they just need much more cooking time. But they won't hold together as well and will probably lack the intensity of flavor of freshly dried beans. Ideally, you should buy your dried beans at the farmers' market or from a small distributor whose stock is constantly being refreshed. Getting to know a bean farmer will also acquaint you with some of the incredible variety now available. For instance, a number of rare heirloom black bean varietals have recently come on the market—Black Calypsos, Midnight Blacks, and Ayocote Negros, to name a few. Try different kinds of beans to find out which you like best and which work best in which dishes. A crumbly bean might be welcome in a soup, but an intact bean would be preferable in a cassoulet.

Beans Cooked over the Fire

Preparing beans this way is entirely worth the extra effort—their earthy flavors are amplified by the smoke.

Soak the dried beans overnight. Drain and put them in a ceramic bean pot or any other flameproof pot. Add fresh water to cover the beans by 2 inches. Add some aromatics: A bay leaf, a couple of garlic cloves, and an onion will do, but adding a chile and epazote sprig will add depth to black or Rio Zape beans; while rosemary and sage complement cranberry and borlotti beans. A piece of cured pork (such as a ham hock or a piece of pancetta, bacon, or prosciutto) can do wonders, too, but isn't necessary if you'd like to keep your beans vegetarian. Sometimes I add a pinch of smoked paprika to a pot of beans once they're fully cooked to give them that extra meaty flavor without actually using any meat.

To cook the beans, build a small fire in the hearth. When it is established, place the bean pot on a stand over the fire. Cook until tender, about 1 hour. When the beans are cooked through, carefully remove and discard whatever aromatics you've added. Season the beans with plenty of salt and cook for a few more minutes. If you feel the beans need a little extra flavor or texture, you can make a fresh mirepoix to add to the cooked beans: Sauté chopped onion, carrot, celery, and a bay leaf in olive oil and cook until tender (about 10 minutes) and then add thinly sliced garlic and a mixture of herbs and cook for a few minutes more. Add a chopped tomato or two to the mirepoix, if you like, and cook an additional 5 minutes. Stir the mirepoix into the beans and add a touch more salt, if needed.

White Bean Crostini

4 TO 6 SERVINGS

This is a lovely and simple snack or light lunch to make when you have extra cooked beans on hand. If cooking the beans from scratch, just soak them overnight and then simmer until tender, adding a sage leaf, a couple of garlic cloves, and, toward the end of cooking, some salt. I like to break up the beans using my mortar and pestle to achieve a coarser texture, but you can also use a food processor or food mill for a smoother spread. You will have about 1 cup of bean spread. The purée also makes a light side dish that works perfectly with lamb.

1 garlic clove, peeled

Sea salt

1 cup cooked cannellini beans

1 tablespoon extra-virgin olive oil, plus more for garnish

1 teaspoon chopped fresh sage

Lemon wedge

12 to 18 thin slices of bread, toasted

Using a mortar and pestle, pound the garlic clove with a pinch of salt until it is a smooth paste. Add the cannellini beans and pound gently to mash the beans to your preferred consistency—I like to mash the beans until they are nearly completely broken up, with just a little texture remaining.

Heat the 1 tablespoon oil and sage in a small saucepan until the sage leaves just begin to sizzle. Remove from the heat and let sit for 1 minute. Add the oil to the beans and blend together. Taste for seasoning and add more salt if necessary.

Just before serving, stir in a squeeze of lemon juice and drizzle of extra-virgin olive oil to garnish. Serve on the lightly toasted crostini.

VARIATIONS

﹅ Substitute different herbs for the sage, such as rosemary or marjoram.

﹅ Try other beans, such as fava beans, or any fresh or dried shell bean.

Hummus with Preserved Lemon

MAKES ABOUT 2 CUPS

No store-bought hummus compares to hummus made from freshly cooked chickpeas. Though it takes a bit of premeditation—the chickpeas need to be soaked overnight—you will be amazed at the bright, fresh, and earthy taste of homemade hummus.

¾ cup dried chickpeas, soaked overnight

1 onion, halved

1 carrot, peeled and halved

A few garlic cloves, peeled but whole

Sea salt

1 dried chile (optional)

¼ preserved lemon, rind only, finely chopped

2 tablespoons tahini

2 tablespoons extra-virgin olive oil, plus more for garnish

1 tablespoon fresh lemon juice

¼ teaspoon cumin seeds, toasted and ground

A large pinch of cayenne pepper

Drain and rinse the chickpeas thoroughly and put them in a pot with the onion, carrot, all but one of the garlic cloves, some salt, the dried chile (if using), and enough fresh water to cover the chickpeas by an inch or more. Bring to a boil and simmer until the chickpeas are quite tender, 1 to 2 hours. Allow the beans to cool in the cooking liquid. Discard the onion, carrot, and chile (if you used one). Reserving some of the cooking liquid, drain the chickpeas.

Make the hummus with a mortar and pestle, such as a big Japanese suribachi, or use a food processor or blender. If using a mortar and pestle, pound the remaining garlic clove and a pinch of salt into a smooth paste. Add the preserved lemon and pound until the lemon has completely mixed together with the garlic. Add the chickpeas and mash until they are broken up. Finally, add the tahini, olive oil, lemon juice, cumin, and cayenne. Mix together until smooth, adding some of the reserved cooking liquid if necessary. If using a blender or food processor, start to purée about half of the cooked chickpeas with a little of their cooking liquid. Add the garlic and preserved lemon and when almost completely puréed, add the tahini, olive oil, lemon juice, cumin, and cayenne and mix until smooth, adding more cooking liquid if necessary.

Taste for seasoning and add more salt, cumin, or lemon if needed. When ready to serve, garnish with olive oil and a sprinkling of toasted cumin or cayenne.

Lentil Soup

4 TO 6 SERVINGS

This lentil soup is inspired by the flavors of Lebanese cuisine. The fresh spinach and chopped cilantro that go in at the last minute, along with the generous splash of freshly squeezed lemon juice, give the earthy lentils a bright, fresh burst of flavor.

1½ cups green lentils

2 tablespoons olive oil

1 small onion, diced

1 small carrot, diced

1 small celery stalk, diced

Sea salt and freshly ground pepper

2 large or 3 small garlic cloves, thinly sliced

1 teaspoon cumin seeds, toasted and ground

¾ teaspoon coriander seeds, toasted and ground

¼ teaspoon cayenne pepper (optional)

2 quarts vegetable, chicken, or beef stock, or water

1 bunch spinach, leaves only, rinsed and roughly torn

Fresh lemon juice

½ cup loosely packed cilantro leaves

Plain yogurt (optional)

Sort the lentils, removing any debris, and rinse thoroughly.

Pour the oil into a heavy-bottomed soup pot and heat over medium heat. Add the onion, carrot, and celery and sauté until tender, 5 to 10 minutes. Season with salt and pepper and add the garlic, cumin, coriander, and cayenne (if using).

Add the lentils and stock to the pot along with a few pinches of salt. Bring to a boil, skimming any foam off the surface. Reduce the heat to a simmer and cook until the lentils are soft and fully cooked, 25 to 45 minutes.

Add the rinsed and torn spinach leaves and cook for a couple of minutes to wilt the spinach. Just before serving, squeeze a good amount of lemon juice into the soup and garnish each bowl with a sprinkling of cilantro. A dollop of yogurt makes a delicious garnish.

VARIATIONS
- Any kind of lentil will do, or you can mix together different kinds.
- For a wintertime variation, instead of spinach, add kale when the lentils are almost cooked through and add cubes of roasted winter squash just before serving.
- In the summertime, peeled chunks of tomato complement the spinach, and basil can be substituted for the cilantro.
- If using beef stock, a richer soup can be made by adding ¼ cup red wine to the mirepoix (onion, carrot, celery mixture) after it has fully softened. Cook the wine down for a few minutes then add the stock and beans. The cumin and coriander might be replaced with thyme, rosemary, or parsley—or a combination.

CHAPTER FOUR

SAVORY
PRESERVES

I will never forget the first time I realized the beauty of a canned tomato. Thirty years ago, my friend John Meis—a long-time Tuscan transplant—sent me a jar that contained a single, perfectly intact, peeled San Marzano tomato. It looked almost too beautiful to eat! But one night, when I was home alone thinking about what to make for dinner, I spied that jar on my pantry shelf. I warmed a little garlic in some olive oil and inverted the jar over the pan—the tomato slipped out and melted immediately into a perfect pasta sauce! This is why one of the mainstays of my pantry is a jar of tomato confit canned in late summer when the many wonderful varieties of tomatoes now available are sweetest and most abundant. They are prepared and canned easily, and a single jar makes a beautiful, virtually effortless pasta sauce.

For me, preserving fruits and vegetables is about carrying the brightness and bounty of one season into those that follow. Good preserves
don't mimic the flavor of a fresh ingredient so much as they offer variations on it. This change in complexion, or character, is especially evident
with one of my favorite things to preserve: the tomato. In the summer,
when tomatoes are irresistible and bountiful, I would never dream of
cooking with canned versions. But in the autumn and winter, there's
nothing more divine than the rich, acidic flavor that a preserved tomato
can add to a dish. This is, for me, the "winter taste of summer."

Tomato Confit

6 SERVINGS

Confit is a French word that means "preserved" and refers to something that has been cooked in oil or sugar syrup. When tomatoes are cooked this way, each one holds its shape, becoming sweet and tender, and the flavor concentrates and intensifies. For a wonderful breakfast, put some tomato confit in a little gratin dish, crack open a couple of eggs over the tomato, and bake at 350°F for about 6 minutes. Or if you have some cooked shell beans or a little leftover meat and some greens, reheat them and spoon over a warmed "confitted" tomato: The dish will be greater than the sum of its parts.

A few basil sprigs	*Sea salt*
6 ripe yet firm tomatoes	*½ to 1 cup olive oil*

Preheat the oven to 325°F.

Scatter the basil sprigs in a deep baking dish just large enough to hold the tomatoes snugly. Core the tomatoes and arrange them cored-side down over the basil and sprinkle with salt. Pour oil into the dish until it comes up to the shoulders of the tomatoes—just over halfway. Bake in the oven, basting them occasionally with oil from the baking dish. The tomatoes are done when they are soft to the touch but haven't lost their shape, about 50 minutes. Remove them from the oven and let them cool. When they are cool enough to handle, slip off the skins. Refrigerate, freeze, or can the tomatoes with their juices and the oil.

Roasted Tomato Sauce

MAKES ABOUT 6 CUPS

This can be used as a fresh sauce for pasta or as an element in many different dishes. When tomatoes are abundant, this is a good sauce to make in quantity to freeze or can. I find that roasting the tomatoes, rather than boiling them, produces a slightly more intense and flavorful sauce. If you are going to pass the sauce through a food mill, there's no need to peel and seed the tomatoes beforehand—the mill will strain out the skins and seeds.

4 pounds tomatoes　　　　　*½ to ¾ teaspoon sea salt*
⅓ cup olive oil

Preheat the oven to 450°F.

For a smoother sauce: Roast the whole tomatoes in a baking dish with the oil and salt, stirring every 15 minutes or so to assist their breaking down. After about 40 minutes, the tomatoes should be completely collapsed. Pass them through a food mill into a bowl.

For a chunkier sauce: Peel the tomatoes by dropping into boiling water for 30 to 60 seconds and then plunging into ice water. Remove the cores and peel the tomatoes, then halve them and squeeze the seeds out into a sieve set over a bowl, reserving the juice. Dice the tomatoes and put in a roasting pan or baking dish. Add the oil and salt and strained tomato juice. Roast, checking every 15 to 20 minutes to make sure the tomatoes aren't "catching," or sticking to the pan and starting to burn. The juice will reduce slightly and the tomatoes will begin to break down, and after about 40 minutes the tomato and juice will blend together to form a loose sauce.

Either sauce will keep in the refrigerator for 1 week. It can also be frozen in small batches or canned.

VARIATIONS

~ Add a handful of chopped parsley, marjoram, or oregano or a chiffonade of basil leaves to the sauce a couple minutes before it is done.

~ Sauté 1 onion, finely diced, in the oil before adding the tomatoes.

~ When tomatoes are out of season, use organic canned tomatoes. Reserving the juices, drain one 28-ounce can of whole peeled tomatoes. Chop the tomatoes coarsely and roast them with the oil, salt, and reserved juice.

~ Add a whole dried chile or a pinch of dried chile flakes for spice.

Roasted Eggplant Caponata

MAKES 4 CUPS

Caponata is a sweet-and-sour Sicilian vegetable stew made with eggplant and tomatoes. Served cold it is delicious as an appetizer, on toast, or as part of an antipasto plate; hot it can be tossed with pasta or served as a side dish for roasted meats or fish. I like this version because the roasted eggplant is very tender and flavorful.

2 medium globe eggplants
⅔ cup olive oil
Sea salt
¾ cup finely diced celery
1 onion, finely diced

1½ cups Roasted Tomato Sauce (page 52, the smoother variety)
⅓ cup green olives, pitted and coarsely chopped
3 tablespoons salt-packed capers, soaked in water and drained
3 salt-packed whole anchovies, soaked in water, drained, filleted, and chopped
¼ cup red wine vinegar

Preheat the oven to 400°F. Line 2 rimmed baking sheets with parchment paper.

With a vegetable peeler, peel the eggplant lengthwise in stripes, removing only about half of the skin. Cut the eggplant into ½-inch cubes. Toss with 4 tablespoons of the oil and 1 teaspoon salt. Spread on the baking sheets and roast until lightly browned and tender, about 40 minutes, checking and stirring every 10 to 15 minutes.

Warm 3 tablespoons of the oil in a heavy-bottomed pan over medium heat. Add the celery and sauté until golden. Remove from the pan and set aside. Heat the remaining 3 tablespoons oil in the same pan. Add the onion and cook, stirring often, until the onion is translucent and has lost its crunch, about 7 minutes. Add the tomato sauce and cook for another 7 minutes. Stir in the roasted eggplant and cooked celery as well as the olives, capers, anchovies, and vinegar. Cook for 10 minutes. Taste and add more oil, salt, or vinegar as desired.

The flavors in caponata concentrate overnight—I think it tastes even better the next day.

VARIATIONS
- ⤳ Garnish with ¼ cup chopped basil.
- ⤳ Garnish with 3 tablespoons toasted pine nuts.

Nana's Chile

MAKES 2½ CUPS

Every fall, I get a precious jar of this delicious chile from my friend Ed's mother, Nana, who lives in New Mexico. When chile season begins, the farmer who grows these special chile varietals has an open house and Ed's whole family goes out to the farm, where chile roasters are set up. Everyone in the community buys chiles, has them roasted, and then seeds them on-site. For this recipe, the roasted and seeded chiles are cut into squares and mixed with raw tomato, onion, and garlic and used as a condiment to spoon over eggs or beans, sauté with rice, or add to the braising liquid for chicken or pork. I love its delicious green chile flavor—Nana always insists, "More green than red!" I make a California version using the beautiful green Anaheim chiles that grow here. Nana makes enough for the whole year and then freezes it in small portions.

12 Anaheim chiles

2 small tomatoes, finely chopped

1 garlic clove, minced

½ white onion, finely diced

Sea salt

Preheat the oven to 450°F.

Arrange the chiles side by side on a baking sheet. Roast, turning the chiles every 5 minutes, until they are blistered and black, about 20 minutes. Use tongs to transfer the peppers to a brown paper bag. Close the bag and let them steam for 10 minutes.

One at a time, put the peppers on a cutting board and slit open vertically with a paring knife. Pull out the stem and as many seeds as possible. Use the knife to scrape out any remaining seeds. Flip the flattened pepper over and scrape off the skin. (Don't rinse the skin off under running water.) Cut the peppers into ½-inch squares. Put the peppers into a medium bowl and add the tomatoes, garlic, onion, and salt to taste. Store in the refrigerator in tightly sealed jars.

All-Purpose Pickling Brine

MAKES ABOUT 3 CUPS

I use this brine to pickle little cauliflower florets, sliced carrots, quartered pearl or cipolline onions, halved okra pods, small turnips cut into wedges (with some stem attached), whole green beans, whole chiles, small cubes of celery, fennel, and winter squash—and more. Sometimes I just slice red onions very thin and pour the boiling brine over them. By the time they cool they will have cooked just enough, and are delicious served with smoked fish and new potatoes or garnishing a smoked salmon toast.

1¼ cups white wine vinegar	A pinch of dried chile flakes
1¾ cups water	½ teaspoon coriander seeds
2½ tablespoons sugar	2 whole cloves
½ bay leaf	4 garlic cloves, halved
4 thyme sprigs	1½ teaspoons sea salt

Combine all the ingredients in a saucepan and bring to a boil. Add small or chopped vegetables to the brine, cooking each type of vegetable separately and removing them when they are cooked but still a little crisp. Remove the vegetables with a slotted spoon and set them aside to cool to room temperature. Once all the vegetables are cooked and cooled, allow the brine to cool as well. Stir the vegetables together gently in a large bowl, then transfer to jars or other covered containers, cover with the cooled pickle brine, and refrigerate. You can keep this basic brine in your refrigerator and reheat it to make fresh pickles when you are inspired by a trip to the farmers' market.

VARIATION
～ Feel free to alter the ingredients of the brine: Try using red instead of white vinegar, or adding a bit of saffron, another kind of dried chile than chile flakes, or slices of fresh jalapeño.

Pickled Young Ginger

MAKES ABOUT 1 CUP

If you can get your hands on tender young ginger, it takes very well to preserving this way. More mature, tougher ginger can be pickled as well, but it is best to blanch the slices in boiling water first. I use a Japanese mandoline to slice the ginger very thin. It is a delicious condiment for rice and vegetables.

4 ounces tender young ginger, peeled and thinly sliced

½ cup rice vinegar

¼ cup water

1½ teaspoons sea salt

4 teaspoons sugar

3 red shiso leaves (optional)

Combine all the ingredients in a small saucepan. Heat gently until the sugar is dissolved. Cool to room temperature, then refrigerate the ginger and brine in a sealed container for at least 4 days. The ginger will keep about 3 months in the refrigerator.

Pickled Sweet Peppers

MAKES ABOUT 2 CUPS

5 small to medium red bell peppers

All-Purpose Pickling Brine (page 57)

Halve the peppers and remove the stems, seeds, and ribs. Cut into wedges or strips. Bring the brine to a boil as directed, then add the peppers and simmer until the peppers are mostly soft but not mushy, about 10 minutes. Let cool in the brine and store in the refrigerator for up to 1 month.

Pickled Wild Mushrooms

MAKES ABOUT 4 CUPS

Of all the wild mushrooms I've tried, little hedgehog mushrooms (*Hydnum repandum*) may be the best for pickling this way.

⅓ cup rice vinegar

⅓ cup Champagne vinegar

2 teaspoons sea salt

2 tablespoons sugar

2 bay leaves

⅛ teaspoon dried chile flakes

4 thyme sprigs

1 pound hedgehog or
    chanterelle mushrooms,
    cleaned and quartered

Combine the vinegars, ⅔ cup water, the salt, sugar, bay leaves, chile flakes, and thyme in a medium pot. Bring to a boil, remove from the heat, and add the mushrooms. Let cool in the brine and store in the refrigerator for up to 1 month.

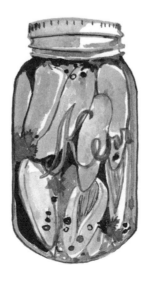

Quick Garlicky Dill Pickles

MAKES 3 QUARTS

Quick pickles are an easy and delicious alternative to traditional fermented pickles. The proportions of pickles to brine may not be exact, depending on the size of the cucumbers and how they fill the jars. It is important to remove any blossoms still clinging to the end of the cucumbers. They are filled with an enzyme that will make the pickles mushy and unpleasant.

25 to 30 cucumbers, 3 to 4 inches long (about 10 pounds)

2 cups white wine vinegar (7% acidity)

6 tablespoons sea salt or kosher salt

1½ teaspoons black peppercorns

1½ teaspoons coriander seeds

3 bay leaves

6 fresh dill flower heads or 6 large tarragon sprigs

3 small dried chiles

6 garlic cloves, peeled but whole

3 fresh grape leaves, rinsed (optional)

Wash the cucumbers well, making sure to remove any blossoms remaining on the ends, and soak in cold water.

Stir together the vinegar, salt, and 1¼ cups water in a medium stockpot and bring to a simmer. Wash and sterilize three 1-quart canning jars with lids by boiling them in water to cover by an inch for 6 minutes. Use tongs to transfer and invert the jars onto a clean kitchen towel to dry and cool slightly.

Into each warm jar, measure ½ teaspoon peppercorns, ½ teaspoon coriander seeds, 1 bay leaf, 2 fresh dill flower heads (or 2 large sprigs tarragon), 1 dried chile, 2 cloves garlic, and 1 grape leaf (if using).

Drain the cucumbers and pack them into the jars. Fill with simmering brine to within ½ inch of the top and seal with lids and bands. Cool to room temperature. Make sure that the lids have made a tight seal once the jars have cooled completely: If they have, the lids should be slightly concave in the center, not flat. If you press down on the center of the lid and it pops back up, the jar isn't sealed. If there are any jars that failed to seal tight, simply store the pickles in the refrigerator and consume them within 4 months to a year. Store the rest in a cool, dark place. Allow them to cure for 1 month before eating. Refrigerate after opening.

Zucchini Pickles

MAKES ABOUT 3 CUPS

These pickles are ready to serve immediately. They are wonderful in a carrot salad or added to a sandwich or a charcuterie plate.

3 medium zucchini

*All-Purpose Pickling Brine
(page 57)*

Cut the zucchini into ⅛-inch-thick slices on a mandoline and place in a bowl. Bring the brine to a boil as directed, then remove from the heat. Let it cool for 3 to 5 minutes and then pour it over the sliced zucchini. Let cool and store in the refrigerator for up to 3 weeks.

Salt-Preserved Kumquats

In Moroccan cuisine, salt-cured lemons are used to add tang and depth of flavor to many dishes. Recently I've been experimenting with salt-curing other types of citrus, too, in particular these rare varieties that have a short season. I especially love salt-cured yuzu, rangpur limes, and kumquats, which are especially good in a kale salad. I often do a simple salt-cure, with salt only, but the recipe below can be spiced up with a bit of coriander, cardamom, clove, and chile. Ginger and star anise also make a delicious variation. Salt-cured citrus fruits make a good addition to relishes, marinades, or sauces. In Vietnam, they're used in a refreshing drink with water and a spoonful of sugar. The citrus becomes quite soft with the preserving and, except for the seeds, the whole fruit is used.

Choose a jar that will just barely fit the quantity of kumquats you have. Wash and dry the kumquats. Sprinkle a ⅛-inch layer of salt in the bottom of the clean jar. I recommend using sea salt or kosher salt for best flavor. Cut a long lengthwise slit down the side of each fruit. Pinch the kumquats open, fill the slit with salt, and pack into the jar. If you would like to add spices, use whole seeds and sprinkle them between every few layers of fruit. Remember that cardamom and star anise are very aromatic and a little goes a long way. Press on the fruits as you add them to help release their juice. If the kumquats don't give off much juice, or not enough to cover them, pour in enough Meyer lemon or other lemon juice to submerge the fruit. Sprinkle another ⅛-inch layer of salt on the top and cap the jar. Let it rest at room temperature for a few days and then store in the refrigerator for a week or two before eating—but you can always sneak a taste before then. They will keep up to a year (they will begin to soften after a few months).

VARIATION
- ~ Follow the same procedure for yuzu, rangpurs, or lemons, making 2 slits in the medium-size fruit and 4 in the larger lemons.

Dried Fig Leaves

The fig tree is one of my absolute favorite plants. Every part of it can be used in cooking: its wood, which lends a fruity aroma to grilled meats and vegetables; its leaves, which can be wrapped around fish, infusing it with a coconut-y flavor; and its jewel-like fruit, perfect eaten sun-warm from the plant, but equally delicious as a savory accompaniment to a roasted duck breast. I display leafy branches in large vases in my kitchen, and I use more fig leaves to line baskets of fruit. One of the things I love about fig trees is that they announce themselves with their perfume. When the weather is either very warm or very wet, their sweet, tropical aroma can be detected from far away. Fig trees are more common in urban land-scapes than most people realize—keep your nose alert and search your neighborhood for your local tree! Even if you live in a climate that won't ripen fruit (like cool, foggy Berkeley), it's still worth planting a tree to use for its leaves and wood.

In the late fall, when the fig trees have shed their leaves, I miss the dis-tinctive verdant flavor they add to many of the dishes I cook, so I figured out a way to preserve them in order to have them always on hand. Once you have a supply you can bake fish or cheese wrapped in the leaves, or use them to infuse crème anglaise.

Wipe both sides of each leaf with a damp towel to remove any dust or debris. Trim the stems with a sharp paring knife, taking care not to cut into the leaf itself. Dry in a 200°F oven for about 1 hour 30 minutes or dry in a dehydrator for 3 to 4 hours. (Or try drying them out on a grill over a very low fire for 1 to 2 minutes on each side.) The leaves should be dry and delicate but not brittle or flaking. Store in an airtight container.

CHAPTER FIVE

WHOLE
GRAINS

I t was only a few years ago that I had something of an awakening
to the deliciousness of whole grains and made the switch from eating mostly "white" grains to mostly whole grains. I have come to
think of our culture's fixation on white food as one of the more perni-
cious facets of Fast Food Nation, because it certainly wasn't always the
case that whole grains were largely absent from the human diet. Whole
grains were around for millennia and were a cornerstone of the diet of
much of the world's population. But after the introduction in 1873 of the
industrial roller mill, the bran and germ could be much more efficiently
separated from its kernel. The result? Considerably less nutritious but far
more shelf-stable foods.

When I switched to whole grains, the greatest revelation was a world of flavor I had been stubbornly resisting for years. Part of this resistance, I suppose, was a vestige of my negative impressions of that first wave of health foods in the 1970s, when the phrase "whole grain" conjured up dense loaves of brown sprouted wheat bread kept in plastic bags in the refrigerator. What I discovered was that whole grains often provide far more depth of flavor than their refined counterparts. As I began trying out different grains to make pasta (farro, barley, whole wheat, corn…), I realized I barely missed the white-wheat versions that had been such a staple of my diet.

This is not to say that I don't still revel in a perfect plate of al dente spaghetti tossed with a little olive oil and black pepper—those perfect Italian pasta dishes will always have their place. But as more consumers have demanded a range of whole grains, more small farms have started to grow a range of interesting older and heirloom varieties of wheat, rye, and barley, which you can now find at some farmers' markets and local grocers. There are also gristmills scattered across the country that source flavorful grains and grind them into delicious fresh flours. Now whole-grain pastas are the only ones I make at home and we serve whole-grain pastas and couscous at Chez Panisse as well.

I especially love the flavor whole-grain flours add to bread, and I per-suaded Steve Sullivan and his Acme Bread Company to develop a 100 percent whole-grain bread for our Edible Schoolyard Project. I've also started using whole-grain flours in other ways at home, where their fla-vors enhance many other baked goods, such as flatbread, crackers, and even some cookies. Pancakes and waffles, too, are so much tastier and more satisfying when made with whole grains that I have absolutely no desire to revisit the white-wheat versions.

It's important to store whole-grain flours properly, because they retain all parts of the grain, including the germ, which contains oil that can become rancid. I recommend buying your flours in bulk from places where you can smell (or even taste) them before purchasing and from small, reliable local farms and gristmills. Whole-grain flours are best stored in the refrigerator in tightly sealed containers.

Because different varieties of wheat contain different amounts of gluten, they behave differently from one another in the kitchen. Experiment with them—it's exciting to see how various different flours change the outcome of a recipe. For example, I've discovered that whole-wheat pastry flour produces crackers, galette dough, pancakes, and cookies that are lighter and less crumbly than those made from all-purpose whole-wheat flour. Pastry flour is made with "softer" wheat (wheat that has less gluten) and is ground much finer; less gluten and finer flour both contribute to lighter, fluffier baked goods.

Corn Tortillas

MAKES 8 TO 10 TORTILLAS

Making fresh tortillas takes a little practice. You have to learn by feel when there is just the right amount of moisture in the masa dough and when a tortilla is cooked—but not overcooked. Once you've learned these things, however, making homemade tortillas is a wonderful skill to have. Traditionally, tortillas are made from freshly ground masa: corn that has been soaked in an alkaline solution, drained, and hulled—a process called nixtamalization—before being ground. The process has been practiced for millennia in Mexico—it makes corn more nutritious and improves its texture and taste. Though you can often find fresh masa at a local taquería, the recipe below uses masa harina, which is flour made from nixtamalized corn. Buy a brand that is organic. Although salt is often not added to tortillas, I add just a little for taste. The most wonderful fresh tortillas are hand patted, but nearly as good are those made in a hinged tortilla press, an inexpensive and easy-to-use tool that makes even, round tortillas. (However, my daughter reports that, in a pinch, she and her friends have successfully used two heavy books instead of a press.)

> *1 cup organic masa harina* *1 cup hot water, or slightly less*
> *¼ teaspoon salt*

In a medium bowl, mix together the masa harina and salt. Add the hot water gradually, stirring with a wooden spoon as you go. Continue adding water until the mixture comes together but is slightly too sticky to handle, using only as much water as necessary. Keep stirring until smooth. Cover with a damp cloth and let rest for 1 hour in a cool place. After this resting period the masa harina will have absorbed the excess moisture and will look smooth and pliable. If it is still a little too sticky, knead in a little more masa harina.

Roll the dough into 1-inch balls (I prefer small tortillas, but you can experiment with size as you get a feel for your press) and cover with a damp towel. Let sit while you heat the griddle(s). You need either a comal (the Mexican name for the cast-iron or earthenware griddles used to cook tortillas) or a large cast-iron skillet. For the best results use 2 skillets, one over medium heat and the other over medium-high heat, or a long griddle that can span two burners, each at a different temperature.

To prepare your tortilla press, cut 2 pieces of parchment paper big enough to cover the inside surfaces of the press. Put one of the pieces of paper on the bottom plate of the tortilla press and place a ball of masa on the center of the paper. Cover with a second piece of parchment and flatten it slightly with your hand. Bring down the top plate of the press firmly, but not with all your force. Open the press and peel off the top parchment paper. Lift the tortilla off the press by the bottom paper, then invert it onto your other hand. Slowly peel off the paper and place the tortilla in the skillet over medium heat. After 1 minute, flip it over into the other skillet. (Or if you are using a single skillet, turn the tortilla and increase the heat to medium-high.) Tap the tortilla gently with your fingertips to encourage the formation of air bubbles that will cause it to puff up. After a minute or so, once the underside is opaque and maybe even speckled brown in a few spots, flip the tortilla over if the first side still appears raw. I try not to flip the tortilla too many times, as it can become tough. When the tortilla is cooked, keep it warm in a clean kitchen towel as you continue pressing, cooking, and flipping the remaining dough balls. Though wonderful when eaten freshly made, tortillas can be wrapped in foil and reheated later in a skillet, or over an open flame.

Store tortillas in airtight containers or bags in the refrigerator for up to 3 or 4 days.

VARIATION

~ One of my favorite things to do with tortillas is to make a light lunch of garden salad tacos. I quickly warm a tortilla over the flame, grate a little Monterey jack or mild cheddar cheese over the top, place it in the oven on a baking sheet until the cheese just melts, and top it with a slice of avocado, some cilantro leaves, and a handful of chopped greens (whatever I happen to have on hand) seasoned and dressed with a little olive oil and vinegar. I also love making a variation of the Mexican breakfast dish called huevos rancheros: I put a fried egg on top of a tortilla lightly fried in oil and spoon over a generous amount of roasted tomato salsa or Nana's Chile (page 56). When I've had tortillas in my fridge for more than a few days, I'll sometimes use them to make delicious, thick tortilla chips. Just cut the tortillas into triangles or long strips and fry them in batches in an inch of peanut oil (or another neutral oil) until golden brown. Drain on paper towels and sprinkle liberally with salt while still hot.

Multigrain Porridge

6 TO 8 SERVINGS

I can't think of a better reason to keep a quantity of cooked brown rice in my refrigerator than this porridge. It makes a wonderfully nourishing and warming breakfast, good for cold mornings. The savory variation below, topped with an egg, also makes a very satisfying lunch.

½ cup millet

¼ cup red quinoa

1 cup cooked brown rice

¼ cup golden raisins (optional)

¼ teaspoon sea salt

Chopped nuts, butter or milk, and maple syrup, for serving

The night before, soak the millet and quinoa together in 2 cups water. In the morning, drain the grains in a fine-mesh sieve and rinse well to rid the quinoa of any bitterness.

In a medium saucepan, combine the cooked brown rice, millet, quinoa, raisins (if using), salt, and 3½ cups water. Bring to a boil. Skim off any foam and then stir, making sure nothing is sticking to the bottom or sides. Cover and simmer very gently until the grains are fully cooked and beginning to break down and the texture is as thick as you like it, 30 to 40 minutes, stirring after 20 minutes and every few minutes thereafter. Add water if it gets too thick. Serve with chopped nuts, a little butter or milk, and maple syrup.

VARIATIONS

~ Add 2 tablespoons of amaranth seed (or any other whole grain) to the soaking grain mixture the night before.

~ Make a savory breakfast porridge by omitting the raisins and finishing with butter or ghee, sea salt, finely chopped chives or herbs, and, if you like, a 6-minute egg.

~ Stir ground flaxseed into the cooked porridge.

Fanny's Superfood Granola

MAKES ABOUT 7 CUPS (1¾ POUNDS)

Part of what encouraged my transition to whole grains was having my daughter, Fanny, a whole-grain and superfood enthusiast, back home from time to time. When Fanny was in college, she came up with the recipe for this granola, which she claims gave her the long-lasting energy she needed to get through a morning of classes. Making granola is not at all complicated and you can easily customize the recipe. The only time-consuming part is stirring it while it bakes to ensure it doesn't burn around the edges. Serve it with homemade yogurt for a delicious and healthy start to the day, or eat it by itself as an afternoon snack.

3 cups rolled oats

½ cup buckwheat groats

½ cup red quinoa

1 cup sliced almonds

1 cup almonds, pecans, or walnuts, coarsely chopped

¼ cup sesame seeds

½ cup chia seeds, ground

½ cup sunflower seeds

½ teaspoon ground cinnamon

½ teaspoon ground cardamom

1 teaspoon vanilla extract

¾ teaspoon sea salt

⅓ cup coconut oil

⅓ cup honey

¾ cup golden raisins

¾ cup unsweetened shredded or flaked coconut

Preheat the oven to 350°F.

In a large bowl, mix together the oats, buckwheat, quinoa, almonds, chopped nuts, sesame seeds, chia seeds, sunflower seeds, cinnamon, cardamom, vanilla, and salt.

Measure the coconut oil and honey into a heavy-bottomed saucepan. Warm over low heat, stirring until combined. Pour half the mixture into the dry ingredients and toss to distribute. Add the remaining oil and honey mixture and toss again until the granola is evenly moistened.

Spread the mixture evenly on a rimmed baking sheet or jelly-roll pan. Bake for 10 minutes, then take the pan out of the oven and toss the granola with a spatula. Return to the oven, removing the pan and stirring every 5 minutes to ensure even toasting, until lightly browned, about 30 minutes in total. Add the raisins and coconut and bake for a final 5 minutes to lightly toast the coconut. The mixture should be golden. Remove from the oven and allow to cool completely.

Store in an airtight container for up to 1 month.

VARIATIONS
- Add ¼ cup of amaranth seed, pumpkin seeds, or flaxseeds.
- Sweeten with ¾ cup maple syrup instead of honey.
- Instead of coconut oil, use clarified butter or a neutral oil.

The Many Uses of Cooked Brown Rice

Until a few years ago, I can honestly say I was a bit prejudiced against brown rice, a grain I associated primarily with the overcooked globs that underlay so many undistinguished vegetarian curries during my college days in Berkeley. The rice grown by Massa Organics, a small sustainable farm near the Sacramento River, has completely changed my opinion of brown rice—it's sweet and nutty and can be cooked slightly al dente. This brown rice is among the most versatile and delicious staples of my pantry; hardly a week goes by without my preparing a large pot to use over the next few days.

To make a large batch, you don't need to obsess over the ratio of water to rice. I simply fill a large pot with plenty of water and cook the rice (amply rinsed in cold water beforehand) as I would dried pasta, draining it in a colander or large sieve once the grain has reached the desired level of tenderness (somewhere between 25 and 40 minutes). Once it's drained, I spread the rice on a large tray or platter and allow it to cool completely. Prepared this way cooked rice will keep in my refrigerator for up to 1 week, ready for me to use in a variety of ways for breakfast, lunch, or dinner.

One of my favorite things to do with cooked brown rice is to reheat it in a pan with a little olive oil and plenty of chopped fresh herbs and serve it alongside a fried egg for breakfast. If I've made sautéed greens the night before, I'll chop those up and add them to the rice as well. For a dinner variation, to serve with braised or grilled meat or roasted vegetables, I'll make this shorthand version of "jeweled rice": Sauté an onion and a minced clove of garlic, then add the rice to heat through and fold in some toasted sliced almonds and a handful of currants at the very end. I also love a quick lunch of hand-rolled brown-rice sushi: Just spread a spoonful of cooked rice across a lightly toasted sheet of nori, add a few slices of avocado and cucumber and a shake of sesame seeds, and roll into a little cone for dipping in a soy–rice vinegar sauce.

Brown Rice and Herb Salad

6 TO 8 SERVINGS

I often make a salad for lunch using cooked rice and whatever vegetables and herbs I happen to have on hand. It is always a little misleading to give exact quantities for a salad like this because it is never going to turn out the same way twice, whether or not you carefully measure out the chopped herbs.

1 garlic clove, peeled

Sea salt

Freshly ground black pepper

4 teaspoons red wine vinegar

½ pound cherry tomatoes

2 cucumbers

2 cups cooked brown rice

¼ cup chopped mint leaves

¼ cup chopped cilantro, leaves and tender stems

¼ cup chopped parsley, leaves and tender stems

⅓ cup extra virgin olive oil

Pound the garlic clove and a pinch of salt into a smooth paste in a mortar. Add some pepper and the vinegar.

Cut the tomatoes in half, peel and dice the cucumbers, and toss the vegetables in a bowl with the rice and chopped herbs. Whisk the olive oil into the vinegar in the mortar and stir this vinaigrette into the bowl with the rice and vegetables.

Serve at room temperature.

VARIATIONS

~ Try other combinations of tender herbs such as basil, chives, or dill.

~ Add some chopped Salt-Preserved Kumquats (page 62) or preserved lemon to the vinaigrette.

~ Add other vegetables: diced fennel or celery, sliced radishes, grated raw golden beets, or chopped leaves of Belgian endive or radicchio.

Buckwheat Buttermilk Crêpes

MAKES 18 TO 20 CRÊPES

I've always loved the flavor of buckwheat. These versatile crêpes are a perfect vehicle to roll around a savory filling such as wilted greens or a dessert filling like sautéed apples. I suggest playing with the ratio of buckwheat to white flour. Increasing the amount of buckwheat flour will make a nuttier, more hearty crêpe; decreasing it will make a milder, sweeter one. You can either fry all the crêpes in one go and reheat them over the next few days, or keep the batter for up to 1 week in the fridge, making a few crêpes at a time as needed.

½ cup buttermilk

½ cup milk

2 eggs

3 tablespoons butter, melted

⅔ cup all-purpose flour

⅓ cup buckwheat flour

1 teaspoon sea salt

In a medium bowl, whisk together the buttermilk and milk. Add the eggs, one at a time, whisking until incorporated. Stir in the melted butter and ⅓ cup water. In another medium bowl, mix together the flours and salt. Make a well in the center of the flour mixture and pour the egg mixture in slowly while whisking constantly. Once all the flour is incorporated into the batter, whisk vigorously for 1 minute. Cover the bowl and refrigerate overnight.

Heat a crêpe pan over medium-high heat. If the pan is not well seasoned, rub a small amount of butter on it, wiping out any excess with a paper towel. Ladle a thin layer of batter, about 3 tablespoons, into the center of the pan, tilting the pan so that the batter spreads as thinly and evenly as possible around the bottom. Lightly brown the crêpe for 1 to 2 minutes, release the edges with a spatula, and flip it over, cooking the other side for about a minute, until browned. Turn the crêpe out onto a plate and, if you wish, hold the finished crêpes in a warm oven as the others cook.

The crêpes may be served as they are, with a little butter and drizzle of honey, or filled with savory or sweet fillings of your choice.

VARIATIONS

- ⤳ For dessert crêpes, add ½ teaspoon vanilla extract to the batter.
- ⤳ To match the assertive buckwheat flavor, drizzle a strongly flavored honey, like chestnut honey, over the crêpes.

Oat Pancakes

MAKES 8 PANCAKES (3 TO 4 INCHES IN DIAMETER)

This is another recipe that my daughter, Fanny, loves to make. We often cook up a small batch together when she visits. Not only are these pancakes a treat, they are actually incredibly wholesome and would make a wonderful breakfast for kids. They are delicious with a dollop of yogurt or cottage cheese and warm berry compote. Making your own oat flour is also unbelievably easy and yields a fresher, sweeter tasting flour than any store-bought variety.

1 cup rolled oats

¾ cup milk or almond milk

1 large egg

3 tablespoons ghee, coconut oil, or butter (or a combination), melted

½ teaspoon sea salt

1 teaspoon baking soda

½ teaspoon baking powder

Put the oats in a blender or food processor and blend until it is a fine powder (this shouldn't take more than 20 or 30 seconds). You will have about ¾ cup oat flour.

Beat the milk and egg together with a fork in a medium bowl. Stir in the melted oils—I like a mix of ghee and coconut oil, which lends both buttery and coconut-y flavor to the pancakes. Add the oat flour, salt, baking soda, and baking powder and stir just until combined. Let the batter sit for 10 minutes to thicken.

Heat a skillet over medium-high heat. Grease lightly with oil or butter and spoon on the batter, about ¼ cup per pancake. Cook the pancakes until a few bubbles on top have broken, then flip them over and cook until golden on both sides.

Whole-Wheat Flatbreads

MAKES 16 FLATBREADS

I developed this recipe because a local farmer began to grow an heirloom wheat variety and I wanted to find a way to use it. The flatbread that resulted falls somewhere between a tortilla and a chapati and has become a staple in my pantry. I often have one for a savory breakfast in the morning, blistered over the burner and spread with a bit of hummus or raita, but it is a welcome snack any time of day served warm with olive oil and za'atar, or any savory spread.

You may have to experiment with different whole-wheat flours before you find one that works well; the one that works best for me is ground very fine and has relatively little bran in it.

2 cups whole-wheat flour

1 teaspoon sea salt

½ teaspoon baking powder

¾ cup warm water, or more

3 tablespoons extra-virgin olive oil

In a large bowl, whisk together the flour, salt, and baking powder. Stir in the water and oil. Knead briefly to form a soft, moist dough. If the dough is too dry, add a little more water. Cover the dough with a kitchen towel and let rest for 30 minutes.

Divide the dough into 16 balls. On a lightly floured work surface, use a rolling pin to roll each ball into a 6 × 3-inch oval.

Heat a 10-inch cast-iron skillet over medium heat. Cook two flatbreads at a time until they start to brown on the bottom, about 2 minutes. Flip and cook until browned in spots on the other side, about 2 minutes more. Wrap the flatbreads in a clean kitchen towel while still warm to let the breads moisten from the steam.

Just before serving, use tongs to hold each flatbread briefly over an open flame, turning until lightly charred on both sides. Serve warm.

Pita Bread

MAKES 16 TO 18 PITAS

This pita bread is similar in flavor to the flatbreads I make, but it's slightly more versatile and substantial. Stuffed with dressed cucumbers and tomatoes and a little hummus, a pita makes a lovely light lunch. They are also delicious with a bit of cheese or nut butter as an afterschool snack for kids.

2 teaspoons active dry yeast	*1 tablespoon sea salt*
2½ cups lukewarm water	*1 tablespoon olive oil*
3 cups whole-wheat flour	*2 to 3 cups all-purpose flour*

To make the sponge: In a large bowl, sprinkle the yeast over the warm water and stir clockwise to dissolve. Mix in the whole-wheat flour, 1 cup at a time, and continue to stir clockwise for another minute or so. Let the sponge rest for at least 15 minutes and up to 2 hours.

To make the dough: Sprinkle the salt over the sponge, add the oil, and mix until combined. Stir in 2 cups of the all-purpose flour, 1 cup at a time. Add more of the remaining flour until the dough is too stiff to stir easily. (I often use less than 3 cups because I prefer a wet dough, which is harder to handle but makes more tender bread.) Turn the dough out onto a lightly floured surface and knead for about 10 minutes, or until smooth and elastic. Rinse out the bowl, dry, and oil lightly. Return the dough to the bowl and cover the surface of the dough with a damp towel. Let rise until doubled in bulk, about 1 hour 30 minutes. (At this point, you could refrigerate your dough, letting it rise in the refrigerator overnight rather than at room temperature.)

Line 3 baking sheets with parchment paper. Divide the dough in half and cover one of the halves with a damp towel. Divide the other half into 8 equal portions (each one will weigh about 3¾ ounces). Roll the portions of dough into round balls one at a time, covering the others with the towel. On a lightly floured surface, gently use your hands to pat each portion into a 5- to 6-inch round about ¼ inch thick. (If you prefer, you can use a rolling pin, but be sure you don't roll the dough too thin, or the bread may not form an air pocket when it bakes.) Place the disks about 1 inch apart on the parchment-lined baking sheets and cover with towels to prevent a skin from forming. Make 8 more pitas with the remaining dough half, and let all the disks proof for about 30 minutes.

Preheat the oven to 450°F. If you have a baking stone, put it in to preheat with the oven on the middle rack; a stone makes the heat more even and intense under the baking sheets.

Bake the breads for 4 minutes without opening the oven. After 4 minutes, flip the pitas over and bake until each pita has puffed up like a balloon, an additional 3 to 4 minutes. Wrap the hot pitas in a clean kitchen towel to let them steam and soften as they cool. If you need to bake more than one batch, let the oven come back up to temperature for 5 minutes before putting the next batch in.

⊱

CHAPTER SIX

PRESERVED
FISH and MEAT

S ometimes deprivation is the mother of inspiration. I remember when I first learned that we would have to do without some kinds of fish because they can be caught sustainably only during the times of year when they are most abundant. The wild Pacific salmon, for example, a mainstay of the Chez Panisse menu, though plentiful between May and September, is out of season the rest of the year. But the limited availability of salmon—and fish such as halibut and albacore tuna, too— inspired us to think more creatively about the other fish that are local to the California coast. We began to feature some of these smaller, more prolific fish; and now sardines, sand dabs, mackerel, anchovies, and cod have as much of a place on our menu—and on my menus at home—as our beloved Pacific salmon does.

Because more and more wild fish populations are in decline, it's important to take advantage of the diversity of fish that is still available. When anchovies and sardines are plentiful and inexpensive, we make a point of salt-curing, pickling, or preserving them in olive oil to use throughout the year. Since these smaller fish are known to contain more omega-3 fatty acids and less mercury and other heavy metals than bigger fish higher up the food chain, we've made a concerted effort to use them more often and find delicious ways of preparing and preserving them. Once you've learned how easy it is to preserve fish for both the short and the long run, you'll find yourself curing anchovies or making your own sardine escabeche or codfish brandade. Extending the life of ingredients and making use of those that are most plentiful are some of the most important and rewarding lessons of the home pantry.

Finding truly organic poultry poses another confusing and difficult problem. For one thing, many organic birds are fed on organic chicken feed from China and India that has to be shipped halfway around the world. One of our most reliable local suppliers, Riverdog Farm in the Sacramento Valley, sells wonderful chickens (the breed they raise for meat is called Freedom Ranger!). Their birds are pastured outdoors and fed organic feed, but this is expensive: The price of a whole dressed chicken is more than three times the average price of a mass-produced factory bird, and this means that a chicken in the pot on Sunday is once again the luxury it used to be. It also means we have to be creative and make the most of every single bird.

A single chicken can be the basis for much more than a single meal. For one dinner, a bird can be cut into pieces, the thighs and drumsticks cut apart, and the legs braised in homemade chicken stock from your freezer; for another, the breasts can be boned and flattened, and fried or grilled; and the leftover wings and the rest of the bones and scraps can be consigned to make more stock. A whole roast chicken will almost always have enough leftover meat on its carcass to turn into a little chicken salad with celery and mayonnaise; and the leftover carcass will also find its way into the stockpot. Making and freezing stock is an unbeatable way to preserve and extend the flavor of chicken—and beef, for that matter— into countless soups and stews.

All the recipes in this chapter are meant to encourage you to use the whole animal. The excess fat on a duck, for example, can easily be rendered and used for frying potatoes or preserving duck legs. Not only is rendered fat a fantastic medium in which to cook and preserve meat for all kinds of dishes, from cassoulets to carnitas, it is wonderful for browning poultry, for adding flavor to a braised cabbage, and for sautéing wild mushrooms—not to mention how delicious it is spread over warm garlic-rubbed crostini.

Sardines Escabeche

MAKES 12 FILLETS

Escabeche is the name for several Mediterranean and Latin American dishes of poached or fried fish that is then marinated in an acidic mixture along with various vegetables. The dish is perhaps most common in Spain, which is where I first tasted and loved it. I find that this recipe is a wonderful way to prepare sardines (or sand dabs, anchovies, and mackerel, too), because the brightness of the pickled vegetables cuts through the oiliness of the fish.

6 fresh whole sardines, filleted, or 12 sardine fillets

2 to 3 teaspoons sea salt

FOR THE BRINE:

1 tablespoon olive oil

½ yellow onion, sliced into thin half-moons

2 garlic cloves, sliced

1 celery stalk, sliced

1 cup Champagne vinegar

1 tablespoon sugar

1 teaspoon sea salt

¼ teaspoon coriander seeds

¼ teaspoon fennel seeds

¼ teaspoon black peppercorns

A pinch of dried chile flakes

2 allspice berries

1 bay leaf

3 to 4 thyme branches

½ cup olive oil

½ cup all-purpose flour

Season the sardine fillets with the salt and let sit at room temperature while you begin the brine.

Make the brine: In a skillet, heat the oil over low heat. Add the onion, garlic, and celery and cook until tender and translucent, about 10 minutes. Add 1 cup water, the vinegar, sugar, salt, and all the spices and herbs. Bring to a boil, turn off the heat, and let cool.

Line a baking sheet with paper towels. Heat the olive oil in a skillet over medium heat. Dredge the sardines in the flour and fry in the hot oil until browned, 3 to 4 minutes. Transfer to the baking sheet to drain and cool.

Once the brine and fillets are both cool, lay the fillets in a container, pour the brine and vegetables over them, and refrigerate. Let sit for a few hours or overnight. The sardines should keep for a week or so in the refrigerator.

Salted Fish

For centuries, salt cod from the North Atlantic was a staple of diets around the world. The big fish were cleaned, split, salted, and dried out-doors in the sun and wind. Once dried, salt cod was easy to transport and trade, and it could be stored unrefrigerated for years. Salt cod became a traditional ingredient not only in Northern Europe, but all around the Mediterranean and the Caribbean, in West Africa, and in Brazil. To be edible, the dried fish had to be soaked for as long as three days in sev-eral changes of water before cooking. Once it was rehydrated and boiled, salt cod formed the basis of many delicious preparations, including the French classic, *brandade de morue*, an emulsified mixture of salt cod, milk, potatoes, garlic, and olive oil.

After many years of using Atlantic salt cod at Chez Panisse, we were told one day it would no longer be available; it had become overfished and the fishery had officially closed. For us, the Atlantic cod was the canary in the coal mine that forced us to pay closer attention to the sustain-ability of our oceans and think about which fish we were putting on the menu. After the Atlantic cod fishery collapsed, we started experimenting with salting local Pacific halibut and lingcod. We continue to do so today at Chez Panisse, but it is a technique well suited to home use, too. Fish salted this way won't keep for months or years—unlike salted dried Atlantic cod—but it will keep for a week or so and can substitute for salt cod in recipes from all over the world. Most any firm, lean white fish will take to salting. It is an excellent way to treat fish you know you will not be able to cook right away.

Choose fresh, sweet-smelling fillets. Scatter a ¼-inch layer of either sea salt or kosher salt over the bottom of a nonreactive dish or pan. Lay the fish on the salt, making sure no pieces are touching one another, and cover the fillets completely with salt. (If you have a perforated dish large enough to hold the fillets in a single layer, such as a broiler pan rack, suspend it over another dish to catch the liquid drawn out by the salt.) Refrigerate the fish for 2 days. Pour off the accumulating liquids after the first day. After day two, remove the fish from the salt and quickly rinse it. Pat the fish dry and put it in a clean dish on a rack covered with a clean towel. Cover with another towel and cover tightly with a lid or plastic wrap. Change the towels every couple of days until they are no longer dampened by the fish. (At the restaurant we don't bother with towels and leave the fish in a perforated pan with a lid in our large walk-in refrigerator; but if you don't use towels the smell of the fish can be quite strong in a small home refrigerator.) The salted fish can be used as soon as it comes out of the salt pack or held for up to 10 days. Before using, soak the fish for 2 hours or longer: The longer the fish has rested in the refrigerator, the dryer and saltier it will have become and the longer it will need to be soaked. The fish is ready when pliable, but don't soak it so long that it becomes mushy. Change the soaking water every hour or so to speed up the process.

Brandade

4 SERVINGS

Brandade is wonderful spread on grilled toasts and served alongside a salad of hearty, vinegary greens—especially mixed chicories. This dish can be a rustic first course or a light meal on its own, served with a glass of chilled rosé and followed by a few perfect pieces of fruit.

1 pound home-salted cod or lingcod, rockfish, or Alaskan halibut (see page 88)

3 cups milk

1 bay leaf

1 medium russet (baking) potato, peeled and cut into chunks

2 to 4 tablespoons extra-virgin olive oil

Remove any bones from the salted fish and soak in water to cover until pliable, about 2 hours, changing the soaking water at least once during the process. Drain and pat dry.

Bring the milk to a gentle simmer with the bay leaf in a saucepan. Add the fish, and poach until tender and just beginning to flake, 5 to 7 minutes. It should not become so flaky that it falls apart in the pot. Remove with a slotted spoon or sieve. Add the potatoes to the same pan and boil until tender, 15 to 20 minutes. Scoop out and pass through a food mill into a bowl.

Flake the fish and add to the potatoes. Slowly pour in the olive oil and mash everything together with a wooden spoon. The consistency should be creamy but not too oily. It shouldn't need more salt, but if it's *too* salty, cook more potato and add it.

VARIATIONS
- ◡ Boil a split clove of garlic in the milk with the bay leaf.
- ◡ Pound a clove of garlic and steep it in the olive oil before using. Pour the oil in first and add the garlic to taste.

Marinated Anchovies

MAKES 50 FILLETS

Anchovies cured this way find many happy uses in my kitchen. Nothing else adds quite that much complexity of flavor at one go. These are ideal for the version of anchoïade I make so often to spread on crostini or to serve with grilled vegetables: a paste of anchovies pounded with dried figs and garlic, fennel and savory leaves, walnuts, and olive oil. These fillets are also wonderful served as a salad with shaved celery, fennel, and red peppers (alone or in combination), sometimes with shavings of Parmesan cheese. And they're good plain, just baked on foil or on toasts for a few minutes in a 350°F oven.

25 fresh whole anchovies

Sea salt

Marash pepper

1 lemon (a sweet Meyer lemon if you have one), very thinly sliced

2 to 4 bay leaves

A few fresh thyme branches

Extra-virgin olive oil

Scale and fillet the anchovies, or ask your fishmonger to do this for you. Season the fillets generously with salt and Marash pepper. Layer the fillets in a dish with the lemon slices, bay leaves, and thyme branches. Drizzle olive oil over them, turn them over, and drizzle again to coat the fish evenly. The fillets are ready after a few hours, and will keep for up to a week in the fridge.

VARIATION

ᴦ This recipe works well for sardines, too. Six sardines are roughly equivalent to 25 anchovies.

Gravlax

6 TO 8 SERVINGS

Gravlax—salmon cured for a couple of days with salt, sugar, pepper, and dill—is a Nordic classic: delicious by itself or on buttered brown bread, sliced thin with a little lemon juice, or with cucumbers, or with crème fraîche and horseradish.

1 pound skin-on salmon fillet	*½ teaspoon black peppercorns, crushed*
¼ cup sea salt	
¼ cup sugar	*A few dill sprigs, thick stems removed*

If the salmon fillet contains pin bones, which run from the head end about halfway back along the side of a salmon, they will need to be removed, as they interfere with slicing the gravlax. They can be easily located with your fingertips and pulled out with small needle-nosed pliers or tweezers.

Place the fillet in a stainless steel or glass dish, skin-side down. In a small bowl, combine the salt, sugar, and crushed peppercorns. Spread the mixture evenly on both sides of the salmon and scatter the dill sprigs on top. Wrap the salmon tightly in cheesecloth, placing a weight on top of it (a saucer will do). Cover the container and refrigerate. After a day, flip the salmon over to ensure that it evenly absorbs any liquid that's been drawn out of the fish by the curing mixture. Cover and return to the refrigerator. The salmon will be ready after 48 hours. If you prefer a saltier gravlax, you can let the salmon cure for another day or two.

When ready to serve, remove the cheesecloth, wipe off any excess seasoning, and slice at an angle into thin slices with a sharp, thin-bladed knife. Stored in an airtight container, it will keep for 1 week in the refrigerator.

Tuna Confit

MAKES 1 POUND

This is infinitely better than canned tuna. We make it only during the short period of the year when we're able to get line-caught albacore tuna. The tuna you use should be as fresh as possible, sustainably fished, skinned, and trimmed of its blood line (the band of strong-tasting, deep-red fatty tissue that runs the length of the fillet next to the skin). Try some crumbled tuna confit with a little aïoli, or in a salade niçoise.

1 pound tuna, preferably albacore, skinned and blood line removed

2 to 3 teaspoons sea salt

½ teaspoon coriander seeds, toasted and ground

½ teaspoon fennel seeds, toasted and ground

¼ teaspoon cracked black pepper

A pinch of Marash pepper (or another ground chile pepper)

2 cups olive oil, or enough to cover the fish

1 garlic clove, peeled and halved

Season the tuna with the salt, coriander, fennel, black pepper, and Marash pepper. Let it sit at room temperature for 5 to 10 minutes.

In a deep pot just big enough to hold the tuna, heat the oil and garlic over low heat just until it is too hot to touch. Cook the fish in the oil for 2 to 3 minutes. (If the tuna isn't covered, add more oil.) If the oil starts to simmer, remove the pot from the heat until it subsides (the fish will continue to cook). Turn the tuna over and cook to medium-rare nearing medium (pierce the fish with a knife to check the center), another 2 to 3 minutes; it will finish cooking as it cools. Remove from the heat and transfer the fish to a platter while the oil cools. When both the fish and the oil have cooled, put the fish in a deep container and pour the oil over the fish. Stored in the refrigerator, it will keep for up to 5 to 6 days.

Rendering Fat:
Lard, Duck Fat, and Ghee

When I am trimming a large piece of pork or a couple of ducks before cooking them, I often set aside the excess fat to be rendered and preserved for many uses. Both lard (pork fat) and duck fat are delicious to cook with and they have relatively high smoke points, which makes them versatile and useful in a variety of dishes. They can also be stored in the refrigerator for quite some time.

I prefer to render fat on the stovetop. The easiest way is to cut the fat into 1-inch pieces and put them in a heavy-bottomed pot. Add ¼ to ½ cup water to the pan, depending on the quantity of fat. (The water prevents the fat from burning before it begins to melt.) Heat steadily over a low flame, checking the pan often, as you want the fat to render slowly. By the time the fat is completely melted, all the water should have evaporated, and the solid remains will have settled to the bottom of the pan and just started to brown—a process that takes about 1 hour, depending on the volume. At this point remove the pan from the heat and let cool. While the rendered fat is still warm, strain it through a layer of cheesecloth into a jar and seal. The fat can be stored in the refrigerator indefinitely. The strained remains can be crisped in a little more fat until golden brown. Called cracklings, they make a delicious snack; and they are also perfect for garnishing a salad of bitter curly endive.

Ghee is a kind of clarified butter used in Indian and Pakistani food to add depth to all kinds of sweet and savory foods. Ghee is traditionally made from cultured cream that is churned into butter and slowly simmered. It is easy to make at home. Start with a pound of organic unsalted butter, preferably the kind made from lightly fermented cream, which will be labeled "cultured" or "European-style." Melt the butter over medium-high heat in a heavy-bottomed saucepan until the butter liquefies and is just beginning to boil. Reduce the heat to a slow simmer. The milk solids will begin to separate from the fat and foam will rise to the top. Do not remove the foam, as you want it to caramelize in the butter and sink to the bottom of the pan. The simmering butter will crackle and sputter as the water evaporates. Let it simmer for 1 hour, keeping the flame as low as possible and checking frequently to make sure the ghee is toasting, not burning. When the caramelized milk solids fall to the bottom of the pan and the liquid above is clear, the ghee is finished. Let cool slightly and then strain into a jar through a sieve lined with cheesecloth. Cover when cool and store at room temperature indefinitely.

Duck Leg Confit

6 SERVINGS

I will never grow tired of duck confit, a dish we've been making at Chez Panisse since the very beginning. At home I make and store duck confit in single-portion containers. Nothing makes a more satisfying meal for one. I like to eat mine with a sharp-tasting salad made of chicories dressed with red wine vinegar. A little bitterness and acid make a perfect foil for the confit's rich, luxurious taste. A few crispy potatoes make a good accompaniment, too.

6 duck legs (thigh and drumstick)

2 to 3 teaspoons sea salt

Freshly ground pepper

Leaves from 4 to 5 thyme sprigs

About 6 cups rendered duck fat (see page 94)

Trim any extra fat from the duck legs and make a cut through the flesh all the way around the "ankle." This will keep the skin from tearing as it shrinks during cooking.

Season the meat generously with salt and pepper. The amount of salt should be just enough to make them taste good but not salty: The rule of thumb I follow is about 1 teaspoon of sea salt—a little more if you are using kosher salt—to 1 pound of duck. Layer the duck legs and thyme leaves in a nonreactive pan and cover. Refrigerate for 2 days.

Melt the rendered duck fat in a heavy-bottomed pan large enough to accommodate the 6 legs. Once the fat is completely melted, add the duck legs meaty-side down. They should be almost completely immersed in the fat. (Don't worry if they're poking out a bit—they will render more fat as they cook; if they are more substantially exposed, add more fat to the pan.) Cook the legs over medium heat, stirring gently with a wooden spoon every so often to ensure that the meat isn't sticking to the bottom of the pan. Once the fat begins to bubble, turn the heat down to low and cook at a bare simmer. Keep an eye on the pot, making sure the fat never comes to a hard boil. The legs are done when the meat is tender and the knee joint moves freely. This will take about 2 hours, but start checking after 1 hour 30 minutes.

Remove from the heat and gently take the legs out of the fat one by one, handling them carefully by the ankle bone rather than by the meat. (The skin is delicate and is likely to tear if pierced.) Cool skin-side up on a rack set over a tray, taking care that the legs are not touching. When the legs are cool, transfer them to a heatproof container and carefully ladle the still-liquid fat over them. There will be some cooking juices at the bottom of the pan, under the fat. Be sure not to ladle any of these juices into the container, or the legs will not keep for as long. (For convenience, the legs can be stored separately in smaller containers to use for a number of meals.) Store in the refrigerator.

When ready to use, place the container in a shallow bath of hot water and simmer until the legs are easy to remove from the hardened fat. Don't tug too hard or the tender legs will tear apart.

Heat the legs in a cast-iron skillet, skin-side down, over medium heat, until browned and crispy. Turn and cook for a few minutes more until warmed through.

VARIATIONS

- ~ Melt the fat on the stovetop in a flameproof baking or roasting pan, add the legs, and once the fat has just come to a boil, put the pan in a 250°F oven to cook. The legs may take longer to cook, but this way the fat is held at a constant temperature.
- ~ Duck wings and gizzards (and the legs, wings, and gizzards of turkeys and chickens, too) can all be made into confit the same way.

Beef Broth

MAKES ABOUT 3 QUARTS

There are a few sauces, soups, and braised dishes that are impossible to make without good, carefully made beef broth. I don't make beef broth routinely at home, but every once in a while it is a deeply satisfying thing to do, especially with the bones of organic, grass-fed beef. Your butcher should be able to provide meaty shanks if you request them a day in advance. Just be sure to request that the shank bones be cut into 2-inch pieces for easier handling.

4 pounds meaty beef bones, preferably shanks, cut into 2-inch pieces

2 carrots, peeled and cut into large pieces

2 onions, cut into large pieces

2 celery stalks, cut into large pieces

1 leek, cleaned and cut into large pieces (optional)

A few black peppercorns

3 thyme sprigs

A few parsley sprigs

1 bay leaf

A few mushrooms, fresh or dried (optional)

2 tomatoes, quartered (optional)

Preheat the oven to 400°F.

Arrange the bones on a heavy-duty baking sheet or in a roasting pan and roast until browned, about 25 minutes. Turn the bones over and add the carrots, onions, celery, and leek (if using) to the roasting pan. Roast for another 25 minutes. Transfer the bones and vegetables to a large pot.

Add the peppercorns, thyme, parsley, and bay leaf (and the mushrooms and tomatoes, if using) to the pot. Cover with 1 gallon cold water. Bring to a boil over high heat, skimming off the foam that rises to the surface, and reduce the heat until the liquid is just barely simmering.

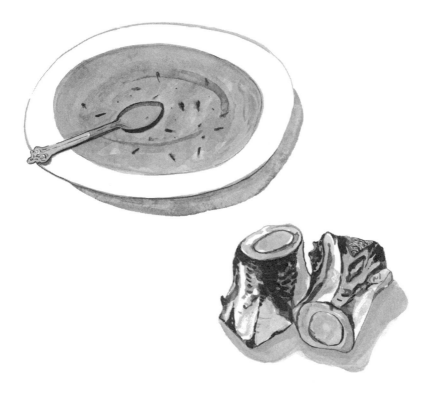

Simmer for 6 hours, checking often to skim off impurities rising to the surface and adjusting the heat to make sure the broth doesn't come to a boil. Add more water if the level of the liquid drops below the level of the bones.

When it's done, carefully strain the broth into a large bowl, discarding the bones and solids, and skim off as much fat as possible. Cool to room temperature before covering. Store in the refrigerator for up to 1 week or freeze for up to 2 months.

Chicken Stock

MAKES ABOUT 5 QUARTS

There are few things more indispensable to me than a good chicken stock. If I don't have a generous supply in my freezer, I'm likely to be simmering a fresh pot on the stove. I don't think I've ever thrown away the remnants of a chicken dinner, or the carcass of any roast fowl—it all goes straight into a stockpot with a handful of aromatics to be turned into a fragrant stock. But when I'm back home after being away for a little while, and I want a fresh batch of chicken stock simmering on the stove to warm up the kitchen and give the house a lived-in feeling, that's when I make the purest and plainest chicken stock, with a whole bird. It's always the first thing I make if I'm staying somewhere new. A beautiful stock is both one of the most versatile ingredients you can have on hand and the sine qua non of certain dishes such as risotto and pasta *in brodo*.

1 whole chicken, or meaty chicken parts (about 4 pounds)

1 carrot, peeled

1 onion, peeled and halved

1 celery stalk

1 head garlic, halved (optional)

1 leek, halved and rinsed

1 teaspoon sea salt

A few black peppercorns

A few parsley sprigs

A few thyme sprigs

1 or 2 bay leaves

Put the chicken in a large pot and add 1½ gallons cold water. Bring the water to a boil over high heat, then turn the heat down low so that the broth is barely simmering, with bubbles just breaking the surface. Skim off the foam that rises to the top, but leave some of the fat as it adds lots of flavor to the stock and can be removed at the end. For a nice clear stock, don't let it boil again, or the fat and the liquid may emulsify, turn-ing the stock cloudy and greasy. After skimming, add the vegetables, salt, peppercorns, and herbs and continue to simmer for 3 to 4 hours (if you're in a hurry, you can use the stock after about an hour, before it is fully cooked). Turn off the heat, let the stock cool a bit, then strain, discarding the solids.

Ladle the stock through a fine-mesh sieve into a nonreactive con-tainer, or several small containers, for freezing. If using the stock right away, skim off the fat. Otherwise, let the stock cool and refrigerate it with the fat, which will solidify on top and can then be easily removed before you use it. The stock will keep, covered, in the refrigerator for up to 1 week or for several months in the freezer.

CHAPTER SEVEN

CHEESE

There are few things better than the taste of fresh homemade cheese, as you'll soon discover. In my early twenties I traveled to Turkey with a friend, and we spent a few days camping near some goatherds and their goats. Every morning we woke to discover either a still-warm bowl of goat's milk or a freshly made goat cheese slipped under the flap of our tent. I will never forget the sweet, tangy flavor of that milk or the perfect simplicity of that beautiful cheese—and most of all, I will never forget the irrepressible generosity of those goatherds. Humans have been herding and milking ruminant animals for so long, and in so many places, that it is no surprise that the offer of fresh homemade dairy products is a ritual of hospitality all over the world.

Just as I learned the meaning of hospitality thanks to those Turkish goatherds, I learned the full meaning of *terroir* when Jean-Pierre and Denise Moullé led my eleven-year-old daughter and me high into the Pyrénées to a small mountainside hut where we watched a shepherd make fresh sheep's-milk cheese with that morning's milk. The smells of the lush wet grass and the sheep and the crisp clear air all found their way into that cheese, which we tasted with delight as the steam from its warmth rose up around our faces. Before that trip I never knew how much eating a cheese could be like having a conversation with the land.

But you don't have to be a herdsman to make delicious cheese yourself, and there are several kinds of fresh cheese you can make easily at home. Experiment with the milk of cows, sheep, or goats. You may find that you strongly prefer the flavor of one type of milk.

Jean-Pierre and Denise also introduced me to the shop of the famous Bordeaux *affineur,* Jean d'Alos. The job of the affineur is to age and care for traditionally made cheeses—the kinds you cannot easily make at home—in special humidity-controlled cellars until the cheeses are perfect for consumption. Depending on what kind they are, they must be aged, dried or moistened, rotated or turned, and in some cases washed with special solutions to encourage certain developments in flavor and texture. From the affineur I learned some important lessons in connoisseurship: For one, that you should always taste the interior of the cheese first and then its rind. The rind is there to protect the cheese— sometimes it is delicious, but sometimes it's a little funky. (If the rind is good, though, serve the cheese with its rind.) I also learned that one must always cut a cheese in a way that honors its shape, so each person gets a bit of both the interior and the rind.

Wherever you live, I encourage you to develop a relationship with any local artisanal cheesemakers. Support them, learn where they get their milk, and how they make their cheeses. One of my dearest hopes is that a cheese producer near me will learn to produce organic mozzarella curd sustainably, for rolling mozzarella at home. Nothing is more delicious than a warm ball of fresh mozzarella!

Making Fresh Cheese

Making fresh cheese is very simple. It requires no unusual ingredients or special places in which to age the cheese. The process simply involves heating milk and adding acid to curdle it. The curds will cling together and separate from the clear, yellowish liquid called whey, which is drained off. The curds become the cheese. They can be eaten while still soft and tender, as with ricotta, or pressed to make firmer cheeses such as ricotta salata and paneer.

There are a few important things to keep in mind when making your own cheese:

~ Use only fresh, organic milk.

~ Don't use ultra-pasteurized milk, because the milk proteins are denatured by the high-heat ultra-pasteurization process and will not bind with the acid to form curds. If ultra-pasteurized milk is the only organic choice, choose fresh milk from a small local dairy instead.

~ Whole milk will make the most flavorful cheese.

~ Some cheeses require the addition of a starter culture consisting of the specific bacteria suited to making a certain kind of cheese. Ordering starters online may seem like a bit of a hassle, but you can store them in the freezer to have on hand for whenever you have an excess of milk or cream, or feel like making cheese, crème fraîche, or yogurt (using a different type of starter for each).

~ Use a stainless steel, enamel, or other nonreactive pan. The cheese is so mild that other flavors will be picked up from more reactive materials such as aluminum and cast iron.

⤲ Have an instant-read thermometer at the ready—it will help you keep track of the temperature of the milk.

⤲ You can line your sieve with ordinary cheesecloth, but butter (or cheese) muslin, which has a finer weave, is preferable. You can find butter muslin at a kitchen supply store or your local fabric store. Wash and dry the muslin after using and save it for your next cheesemaking session. I also use a little basket-shaped cheese mold (which doesn't need to be lined) for ricotta. It makes a beautiful cheese to present as an hors d'oeuvre.

⤲ The cheese is ready to eat once it has been drained, or it can be left to drip for a denser texture, or pressed with a light weight for a firm cheese. Use the whey for baking as you would milk or water—it's incredibly nutritious. Or feed it to your chickens, if you have some; they love it.

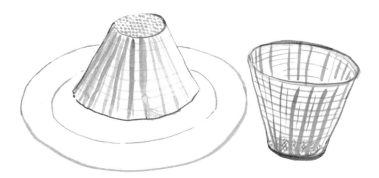

Farmer's Cheese

MAKES ABOUT 3 CUPS

This is a very easy and delicious way to use up extra buttermilk. The cheese can be flavored with a little salt, or chives and black pepper, and is lovely crumbled in salads or sweetened and spread on toast.

3 cups buttermilk　　　　　　　*Sea salt (optional)*

Pour the buttermilk into a 1-quart canning jar and put the lid on tightly. Place the jar in a pot and cover with enough water to keep it submerged. Heat over medium-high heat until little bubbles appear on the jar and in the water, but before the water reaches a boil. Turn off the heat and let the buttermilk cool in the pot until the water reaches room temperature.

Meanwhile, line a nonreactive sieve with a few layers of cheesecloth, or a single layer of butter muslin, and set it in a nonreactive bowl deep enough that there is an inch or two between the sieve and the bowl.

Once the water has cooled, remove the jar of buttermilk and pour the contents into the sieve. You should have firm white curds. You can add a pinch of salt to the curds at this point, if you wish. Cover the curds with the tails of the muslin and refrigerate the sieve over the bowl for 12 to 24 hours, depending on how soft or crumbly you like your farmer's cheese. I drain mine for about 16 hours, at which point the cheese is still soft enough to spread, but dry enough to crumble onto salads.

Ricotta

MAKES ABOUT 1½ CUPS

Homemade ricotta cheese is especially good when still fresh and warm. Pour some olive oil over it, serve with toasted bread, and it will be gone before you know it. It makes a creamy topping for pizza or a light filling for ravioli and it is wonderful in salads paired with tomato or smoky grilled eggplant. Some recipes for ricotta use lemon juice and some citric acid, but I like to use distilled vinegar. It contributes the least flavor to the cheese and produces a cheese that tastes the most like fresh milk.

4 cups whole milk (not ultra-pasteurized)

1½ tablespoons distilled white vinegar

¾ teaspoon sea salt

Heat the milk in a heavy-bottomed nonreactive pot over medium heat until the temperature reaches 190°F. Stir the milk now and then to keep it from scorching. Pour in the vinegar, stir briefly, and bring the temperature back up to 190°F. The milk should coagulate and separate into white curds and lighter colored whey. If this does not happen, add a bit more vinegar, ½ teaspoon at a time. Turn off the heat and let sit undisturbed for 10 minutes.

Place a sieve over a large bowl and line with a few layers of cheesecloth, or a single layer of butter muslin. Gently ladle the curds from the pot into the cloth-lined sieve with a slotted spoon. Slowly stir in the salt. Drain for a few minutes, or longer if you prefer a firmer ricotta. Taste a little to judge the texture. Eat right away or refrigerate for up to 4 days.

VARIATIONS
- For a richer cheese, replace ¼ cup of the milk with heavy cream.
- For a firm cheese, drain, fold the cloth up over the cheese, place a weighted plate on top, and refrigerate in the sieve for 24 hours.

Chèvre

MAKES ABOUT 2 CUPS OR ¾ POUND

To make fresh goat cheese at home, I use a starter from the New England Cheesemaking Supply Company, which is available online. (This company also sells a variety of cheese molds, including ones especially for goat cheese.) One of the nice things about this particular brand of starter is that it includes the necessary rennet so that you don't have to add it separately. When making chèvre, heat the milk at a slow, steady rate, as too much heat destroys the milk proteins that form into curds. If you have an unreliable burner, I suggest using a double boiler to mitigate the uneven heat source. I also find that making cheese late in the day is more convenient, given the time it takes to ripen the cheese and strain it. This cheese is delicious with fresh herbs, marinated in olive oil, or served as a mild breakfast cheese with honey or apricot preserves.

8 cups goat's milk, raw or pasteurized (not ultra-pasteurized)

¼ teaspoon C20G powdered goat cheese starter culture

¼ teaspoon sea salt (optional)

Heat the milk in a heavy-bottomed nonreactive pot over low heat, stirring often, until it reaches 86°F. This should take 10 to 15 minutes; heating the milk slowly will keep the proteins intact. Sprinkle the culture over the top and let sit for 2 minutes. Stir gently a few times in a figure-eight pattern to incorporate the starter. Cover the pot with a lid or plate and place somewhere quite warm (72° to 78°F). Let the milk ripen for 12 to 16 hours. If your oven is well-insulated, this is a good place to store the milk. If it's too cool, first wrap the pot in a thick towel for insulation, or leave the oven light on.

After 12 hours or so, the milk should have formed a firm, but silky, white mass of curds floating in clear whey. Line a nonreactive sieve with a few layers of cheesecloth, or a single layer of butter muslin, and set it over a nonreactive bowl. Gently ladle the curds into the sieve and let drain for 10 minutes. At this point, if you wish to add salt, sprinkle it over the curds and gently toss. Taste, and add more if necessary. Fold the cheesecloth over to cover the cheese in the sieve and let drain for 6 hours at room temperature, flipping the cheese midway through the process. Or if you are using molds, transfer the curds to molds and set the molds over a pan to catch the whey as they drain. The cheese should be creamy after 6 hours and perfect for spreading on toast or adding to a salad. If you like a firmer cheese, continue to drain until the desired consistency is reached. Fresh goat cheese will keep in the refrigerator for 4 to 5 days.

Yogurt

MAKES 6 TO 8 CUPS

Making your own yogurt might seem like a fiddly task, given that good organic brands are now widely available. Still, there's nothing like the magic of transforming milk into creamy homemade yogurt—not to mention how much less expensive and wasteful it is than constantly having to buy it in plastic containers. When I was in my twenties I was so enamored of the process of making yogurt, I must have eaten enough on a weekly basis to feed a family of four. It remains a staple of my pantry to this day. I especially love to use yogurt as a base for quick savory sauces, in condiments like raita, or simply drizzled with honey for a quick little snack or humble dessert.

Yogurt can be made either using a starter culture from a source like New England Cheesemaking Supply Company or from another batch of yogurt. I like both methods, but using the starter culture allows me to make yogurt anytime I have an excess of milk, whether or not I have yogurt in the fridge. You can opt for starters that yield tangy or creamy yogurt, depending on your preference.

Yogurt needs to sit in a warmer environment than the chèvre (close to 110°F). My oven is not that warm, even with the oven light on, but if I heat the oven briefly, turn it off, and then wrap the yogurt in a thick towel, the yogurt thickens quite well. Of course, there are also a number of inexpensive and very straightforward yogurt-makers for sale in cooking shops and online. Using one will take some of the guesswork out of the process, but I don't find them to be necessary for successful home yogurt-making.

6 to 8 cups goat's, sheep's or cow's milk, raw or pasteurized

1 packet yogurt starter (creamy or tangy)

Warm the milk in a heavy-bottomed nonreactive pot over low heat, stirring often. (If your heat source is uneven, use a double boiler.) When the milk reaches 185°F, remove the pot from the heat and let cool to 112°F. At this point, I whisk the milk frequently to help it cool more quickly.

While the milk is cooling, locate a warm spot for your yogurt to sit for 6 to 12 hours. It should be around 110°F. (Heating the oven to 400°F for 10 minutes, then turning it off should create the proper environment.)

When the milk has cooled to 112°F, sprinkle the starter over the milk and let it sit for 2 minutes. Stir gently to dissolve. When the cultured milk has cooled slightly, to about 110°F, cover the pot with a lid, and wrap in a thick towel to insulate it. Place in the oven or other warm spot for 6 to 12 hours, or until the yogurt is thick and creamy. The longer it sits, the tangier it will be. The yogurt can be refrigerated and enjoyed for many days, and it can also be strained to make labneh (see page 114).

Labneh

Labneh is made by draining yogurt to make a cheese that's essentially a firmer version of Greek yogurt. It is a staple of eastern Mediterranean cuisine and is delicious drizzled with olive oil and sprinkled with za'atar, served alongside some slices of cucumber and tomatoes for a quick savory breakfast. Don't discard the whey that is produced as the yogurt drains. Save this wonderful byproduct for cooking. I like to soak bulgur in this whey to plump it up and give it a slight tang. Sometimes I add a couple of tablespoonfuls of whey to my porridge grains as they soak overnight. Or you can use it to feed the plants in your garden.

Line a nonreactive sieve with several layers of damp cheesecloth or one layer of butter muslin and place over a nonreactive bowl with a couple of inches of clearance between the sieve and the bottom of the bowl, enough room for the whey. Use homemade or store-bought yogurt. Spoon the yogurt into the sieve and cover with the tails of the cheesecloth. Put the sieve and bowl in the refrigerator and let drain for 12 to 24 hours, or until the labneh is as thick as you like it. Save the whey.

For a smooth, glossy consistency, remove the labneh from the cheesecloth, put it in a bowl, and whisk vigorously with a teaspoon or two of the whey.

Crème Fraîche

MAKES 4 CUPS

Crème fraîche is often described as French sour cream. This is a helpful comparison, but in fact, crème fraîche's distinctive flavor comes from a different culture altogether. Like yogurt, crème fraîche can be made from other cultured dairy products such as buttermilk. However, using a starter from the New England Cheesemaking Supply Company produces a creamier and tangier crème fraîche. It is quite simple to make and it's a versatile ingredient that I use often to make ice cream, to enrich soups, to spoon over oatmeal, as a base for creamy dressings, and as a garnish for desserts. Swapping it for the milk or cream in recipes like pancakes and biscuits will add tenderness and impart a slight zippiness. You can make crème fraîche with either light cream or half-and-half. Both work quite well; of the two, the light cream's higher fat content makes it the richer version.

*4 cups light cream or
half-and-half*

*1 packet C33 crème fraîche
starter*

Heat the cream in a heavy-bottomed nonreactive pot over low heat to 86°F. Add the starter culture and let sit for 2 minutes. Stir gently to dissolve. Cover and place in a temperate environment, about 72°F, and let it set for 12 hours, or until firm. Transfer the finished crème fraîche to a jar or storage container and refrigerate for up to 1 week.

VARIATION

꙳ If you don't have a packet of starter, substitute heavy cream for the light cream, and stir in 1 tablespoon of cultured buttermilk for each cup of cream. Cover the container loosely, let sit at room temperature until it thickens, about 24 hours, and refrigerate.

CHAPTER EIGHT

SWEET
PRESERVES

There's really nothing like the taste of a freshly picked peach or a handful of sun-warmed blackberries plucked straight from a bramble. That said, having a number of preserved fruit ingredients at the ready in my kitchen is essential to my pantry, and as delicious as most fruits are fresh, the flavors of some seem to intensify exponentially when turned into a cooked compote or a jam. I look forward each year to a precious jar of my friend Patty Curtan's heavenly Blenheim apricot jam no matter how many apricots I've eaten throughout the summer, or how many delicious apricot galettes I've sampled at Chez Panisse.

Her jam, infused with the *noyaux* she cooks along with the apricots, has a concentrated, honeyed flavor totally unlike the fresh version of the fruit—a flavor I relish all the more if I manage to keep some around until the winter.

Fruit tends to taste best and cost the least when it is most abundant and at its seasonal peak. This is the time to gather fruit in quantity to preserve for the colder months ahead. It is also a time to home in on which varieties you like best. Some might be super sweet and ideal for eating raw, while the flavor of other varieties might be amplified by a bit of roasting and a sprinkling of sugar. We're lucky here in California. Mas Masumoto, for example, grows the most irresistible Sun Crest peaches; and Frog Hollow Farm produces a Flavor King pluot that has come to define Chez Panisse's summer fruit bowl. Our summers would likewise be incomplete without Blossom Bluff Orchard's fragrant Snow Queen white nectarines, Knoll Farm's pale green, garnet-fleshed Adriatic figs, or Bob Cannard's luscious blackberries and boysenberries. And then, of course, there are those indispensable Blenheims, the variety of apricot that elevates the Chez Panisse galette to its zenith and makes Patty's jam taste particularly divine. We look forward to these annual special harvests—preserving these fruits is like taking a perfect snapshot of the summer moment.

Fruit can be preserved for a matter of days or for many months. A perfect solution for ripe fruit that is approaching the end of its prime is to cut it up and heat it with a bit of sugar until it starts to release its juices. This kind of fruit compote is a favorite dessert in my family, either served alone or over ice cream. We like it in the morning, too, on top of pancakes or stirred into a bowl of oatmeal. This type of compote will last up to a week in the refrigerator.

Fruit syrups, jams, and jellies take more effort, but will last much longer. These can be quite manageably made in small amounts, but you can also enlist a few friends to help make bigger batches. Another way to preserve the season's bounty is by making fruit paste, sometimes called fruit cheese, a fruit purée that is cooked until very, very thick and then cooled in a mold or a pan. A slice of quince or apple paste with a piece of cheese makes a lovely finish to a meal. Fruit paste will keep for a few months when refrigerated, and if you make more than your household can eat, a nicely wrapped fruit paste (or, for that matter, a jar of homemade jam or jelly) always makes a wonderful gift.

Raspberry Syrup

MAKES ABOUT 1 CUP

I make this when I've puréed raspberries for something else, such as a sherbet or ice cream. While most people would consider the seeds these recipes generate as compost, you can in fact extract something wonderful from them. This gentle cooking yields an incredibly fresh, brightly colored syrup that is a perfect way to wring out all the sweet flavors from beautiful fruit. I add it to sparkling water along with a squeeze of lemon to make a refreshing drink or to a glass of Prosecco for a summery apéritif. It can also be added to simple fruit desserts to lend depth of flavor, it makes a wonderful glaze for fruit tarts or cakes, and it can be used instead of maple syrup over pancakes.

Seeds and pulp from 2 pints of   ⅔ *cup sugar*
   puréed raspberries

Put the seeds, pulp, sugar, and 1 cup water in the top of a double boiler and gently bring to a bare simmer. Simmer for 15 minutes, then remove from the heat and let sit for 5 minutes more. Strain into a jar and cool completely. Cover and refrigerate for up to 3 weeks.

VARIATIONS
- For a thicker syrup, transfer the liquid to a nonreactive pot and boil until it reduces to the desired consistency.
- Use other berries, such as blackberries or mulberries.

Candied Rose Petals or Mint Leaves

MAKES 50 CANDIED PETALS OR LEAVES

It is very important to taste the rose petals you plan to use, as not all rose petals have good flavor. The ideal petals taste slightly sweet and are full of aroma. Keep the rose stems in water until just before assembling these confections, which can be used to decorate cakes, served as a dessert on a candy plate, or used as a garnish on a sorbet or sherbet. They are especially pleasing with strawberry or blackberry sherbets. I use mint leaves prepared the same way to decorate a cake or to serve as candy.

1 egg white

1 teaspoon water

Sugar

50 organic or unsprayed rose petals (from 3 or 4 roses) or 50 mint leaves

In a small bowl, mix together the egg white and water until the egg white is broken up and slightly foamy. Select a pan large enough to hold the petals or mint leaves in a single layer and sprinkle the pan lightly with sugar. Have a small bowl of sugar ready, too.

Using a small pastry brush, paint each side of a rose petal or mint leaf very lightly but completely with the egg white mixture. Sprinkle each side lightly with the sugar from the bowl, just so there is a dusting one grain of sugar thick on each side. If you coat them too thickly they will be too sweet to eat and will look too crystallized. Place the coated petals or leaves on the pan to dry, taking care that the petals are not touching one another. Let them dry for an hour or two, or longer, depending on the humidity. Store in an airtight container in a cool place for about 2 weeks.

VARIATION

⤳ Any edible flower can be candied this way, as can little clusters of red currants or whole bunches of miniature currant grapes (also known as champagne or Corinth grapes) or gooseberries.

Quince and Apple Paste

MAKES A 12 × 8½-INCH SLAB

This is basically the same sweet fruit paste known throughout the Spanish-speaking world as *membrillo* and savored as an accompaniment to cheese. The white flesh of the quince, too sour and astringent to be eaten raw, turns a beautiful red when cooked. Unfortunately, the quince is now a rare fruit in the United States, and most of the quinces in the marketplace are imported from South America, with an inevitable loss of fragrant immediacy. So if you locate a healthy local quince tree, cherish it. Make sure its fruit is harvested and shared with friends, because nothing compares with the perfume of a just-picked quince.

3 pounds quince, cut into chunks

1½ pounds apples, cut into chunks

1 lemon (or Meyer lemon), cut into 1-inch pieces, plus the juice of 1½ lemons

2¼ cups sugar

Combine the quince, apples, and lemon pieces in a nonreactive pan and pour in about ¼ inch water. Bring to a boil, reduce to a simmer, and cook until very soft, about 20 minutes. Discard the lemon pieces and pass the rest of the mixture through a food mill. Stir in the lemon juice and sugar and cook over medium heat until the purée is reduced to a thick paste (be careful of the hot spattering that is inevitable during this step). Pour the purée into a rimmed baking pan (about 9 × 13 × 1 inch) and spread it into a ½-inch-thick layer to fill the pan.

Preheat the oven to 200°F. Turn the heat off, put the pan of purée in the oven, and leave for 7 to 8 hours. Remove from the oven, then flip the paste over so the stickier side is exposed. Preheat the oven again, turn it off, then put the paste back in. This will dry out the purée slowly; you may need to repeat this step more than once. The paste should be thick, uniform, and sliceable.

Once the paste is sufficiently dehydrated, cut it into ½-inch squares. If desired, just before serving, toss the pieces in granulated sugar to coat them and give a sparkly effect.

VARIATION

∾ Substitute 1½ pounds plums for the quince and increase the apples to 3 pounds.

Candied Citrus Peel

MAKES ABOUT 4 CUPS

Candied citrus peel has been a fixture of the candy plate we serve at Chez Panisse for many years now. I very rarely crave something sweet at the end of a meal (my daughter will tell you that salad filled in for dessert at our house too often), but I do love the clean, zingy flavor of a little bite of citrus peel as a palate-cleansing finish. It's also a wonderful way to make use of citrus peel that might otherwise be discarded after making juice or sorbet. If you find you're only squeezing a few citrus fruits at a time, you can save the peels in an airtight container in the freezer and make a batch of candied peel once you've amassed a quantity sufficient to warrant the effort.

4 oranges or Seville oranges,   *4½ to 5 cups sugar*
   8 lemons or tangerines,
   or 3 grapefruits

Wash the citrus fruit well and cut in half. If using grapefruit, cut into quarters. Juice the fruit and either drink it or reserve it for another use (such as a citrus granita). Put the peels in a medium saucepan and cover with cold water. Bring to a boil over low heat and simmer for 10 minutes. Drain the peels, return them to the saucepan, cover again with cold water, bring to a boil and simmer 10 more minutes. At this point, if candying oranges or lemons, test the peel with the point of a knife. If it is tender, then drain and let cool. If it is not yet tender, drain and repeat the process of covering with cold water and bringing to a boil. If you are using grapefruit or Seville oranges, which have more bitter peels, blanch a minimum of 3 times.

Once the peel has cooled, scrape out most of the white part of the peel with a spoon and discard. Slice the peel into long ¼-inch-wide strips, return them to the saucepan, and add 4 cups of sugar for oranges and lemons or 4½ cups for grapefruits. Add 2 cups water and heat the mixture over low heat, stirring often to dissolve the sugar. Allow the peel to cook slowly in the sugar syrup. Have a candy thermometer ready. When the peel is translucent and the bubbles in the syrup start rising smaller and faster, turn up the heat slightly, and cook the syrup to the thread stage, 230° to 234°F.

Turn off the heat and let the peel sit in the syrup for 30 minutes. Set a wire rack on a baking sheet lined with parchment paper. With a slotted spoon, carefully scoop out the strips of peel and arrange the strips on the rack, not touching one another, to dry overnight. The next day, toss the strips of candied peel with the remaining sugar in a large bowl, separating any strips that stick together. Stored in an airtight container in the refrigerator, candied peel will keep for months.

Panforte

MAKES ABOUT 4 DOZEN 1-INCH-SQUARE CANDIES

Every year just before Christmas, I make a huge batch of panforte so that I can give away parchment-wrapped rounds as holiday gifts. Until you have tried panforte, you cannot imagine how addictive it is. When it has just the right balance of sweetness, nuttiness, and spice, there is no tastier treat. I either cut the baked sheet of panforte into square candies or use a biscuit cutter to cut out disks, and wrap them in parchment paper as gifts. I keep all the odd-shaped pieces left over from cutting rounds in a big jar and offer these delectable scraps, along with a little candied peel or a bit of chocolate bark, for a sweet finish to the end of a meal.

2¼ cups raw almonds

2¼ cups candied citrus peel (¾ cup grapefruit peel and 1½ cups orange or tangerine peel)

¾ cup unbleached all-purpose flour

1 teaspoon ground cinnamon

¼ teaspoon freshly grated nutmeg

¼ teaspoon ground cloves

½ teaspoon sea salt

½ teaspoon grated lemon zest

¾ cup granulated sugar

½ cup honey

¼ cup organic corn syrup

Organic powdered sugar for dusting

Preheat the oven to 300°F. Generously butter and flour a 9 × 13 × 1-inch rimmed baking sheet and set aside.

Toast the almonds until golden brown, about 14 minutes, stirring them occasionally to ensure even browning. Remove the almonds from the oven but leave the oven on. When the almonds are cool enough to handle, very coarsely chop. Chop the candied peel into medium-fine dice.

Measure the flour, cinnamon, nutmeg, cloves, and salt into a large, heatproof bowl and mix well. Stir in the lemon zest, taking care to separate any clumps of zest, and add the chopped peel and almonds.

Measure the granulated sugar, honey, and corn syrup into a heavy-bottomed saucepan. Have a candy thermometer ready. Bring to a boil and cook until the temperature reaches 248°F. Remove from the heat and carefully pour the syrup over the nut and peel mixture. Working quickly, stir the whole mass together with a wooden spoon or heatproof spatula to evenly distribute the syrup. Continue stirring until well mixed. Turn the mixture out onto the prepared pan. It will be rather stiff and difficult to work with; use a lightly oiled spatula or dampened hands to spread the mixture evenly. Bake for 25 to 30 minutes, rotating the pan halfway through. The panforte is ready when it begins to bubble all over, so begin checking after 25 minutes. Remove from the oven and let cool, running an oiled knife around the outside edge so that it will release from the pan later. Once the panforte is completely cool, remove it from the pan and dust heavily with powdered sugar. Store in an airtight container and when ready to serve, slice it into ½-inch-thick pieces or cut it into rounds with a sharp biscuit cutter. Stored in a cool, dark place, panforte will keep for months.

VARIATIONS

- To make the removal of panforte from the pan easier, line the buttered pan with edible rice paper, available at many cooking stores.
- Instead of almonds, use a combination of pistachios and hazelnuts.
- Vary the citrus: The candied peel of lemons and citrons (especially the variety known as Buddha's hand) are both especially good substitutes.
- To make *panpepato*, a variation on panforte, replace ¾ cup of the flour with cocoa. Add ¼ teaspoon freshly ground black pepper and ¼ teaspoon cayenne. I find hazelnuts and candied orange peel work especially well here. Dust with a mixture of cocoa and powdered sugar.

Crab Apple Jelly

MAKES 8 PINTS OR 16 HALF-PINTS

In late July, the crab apple tree at the Edible Schoolyard in Berkeley is laden with rosy red crab apples. Too mouth-puckering to eat raw, the flavorful fruit makes a beautiful, clear red preserve. And because crab apples are especially rich in pectin, they're perfect for a quick-setting jelly. One of my favorite uses for this jelly is as a glaze for tarts—it'll give a beautiful rosy sheen to the baked fruit and pastry.

To make a clear jelly you need to strain the liquid out of the cooked fruit very slowly, through a fine-weave cloth bag suspended over a pot or bowl. You can buy a jelly bag, which often comes with some kind of stand, or you can improvise with a tea towel tied to the legs of an upturned stool or an old pillowcase tied to a hanger on a rod.

5 pounds crab apples
6 cups sugar

2 tablespoons fresh lemon juice

Wash, stem, and quarter the apples—you should have about 10 cups of quartered fruit. Put the cut fruit in a large pot and add enough water to just cover. Bring to a boil and cook until the apples are soft and breaking apart. Have a jelly bag fitted on its frame or otherwise suspended over a ceramic bowl or stainless steel pot. Carefully ladle the cooked apples and their liquid into the bag and let them drip, undisturbed. Avoid pressing the pulp in the bag, as this will result in a cloudy jelly. You should end up with about 9 cups of apple juice. Divide the juice equally between 2 large heavy-bottomed pots. (Cooking in two smaller batches is much easier than trying to do it all at once.) Bring both pots to a boil and add 3 cups of sugar and 1 tablespoon of lemon juice to each.

Boil, skimming off any scum that rises to the top, until the temperature registers 220°F. Put eight 1-pint or sixteen ½-pint jars in boiling water for 6 minutes to sterilize them. The screw bands should be washed and rinsed and the snap lids heated in hot water (180°F). Fill the hot jars, wipe the rims clean, and cap with lids and screw bands. Allow to cool and seal. Sealed jars stored in a cool, dark place will keep for 1 year. Refrigerate after opening.

Mary Jo's Brandied Cherries

Because the season for cherries always seems so short, I especially love recipes that allow me to keep some for later in the year. I fold them into vanilla ice cream with a little bit of their juice, or spoon a few over crème caramel or panna cotta. They also make a lovely accompaniment to roasted meats and fowl. And by all means, drink the brandy—it gets better the longer it's flavored by the cherries.

Start with the best cherries and the best brandy you can afford, or use kirsch if you prefer the flavor. This method works for either sweet or sour cherries, but steer clear of soft or overripe fruit. Cherries preserved unpitted and with stems on have the best flavor and are pretty served whole. Cherries to be used for such things as ice cream are better preserved after being stemmed and pitted; save the pits to put in the bottom of the brandy jar for more flavor.

For each pound of cherries, mix 2 cups brandy or kirsch with ½ cup sugar. Add a few more tablespoons of sugar per pound of cherries if you have doubts about their sweetness; for sour cherries, use ¾ cup sugar per pound. Rinse the fruit in cold water, drain well, and stem and pit them, if desired. If you leave the stems on, you can trim them quite short. Put the cherries in a 1-quart jar with a tight-fitting lid. Stir the brandy mixture and pour over the fruit. Cover tightly and keep in a cool part of the kitchen or in the cellar for at least 1 month before using. For the first week, turn the jar upside down daily to help dissolve the remaining sugar crystals. Refrigerate after a month. The cherries will keep for several months.

Preserved Apricots in Syrup

MAKES 2 QUARTS

Apricots are easy to preserve in a light syrup. I add an apricot kernel or two to each jar, for flavor, and a little bit of pure ascorbic acid, to preserve the bright orange color of the fruit. Pure ascorbic acid may be found wherever vitamins are sold.

1½ cups sugar

3 pounds organic apricots,
    washed and well drained

½ teaspoon pure ascorbic acid

Measure the sugar into a medium pot and add 3 cups water. Bring to a boil, stirring to dissolve the sugar. Remove the light simple syrup from the heat and set aside.

Sterilize two 1-quart jars in a large pot of boiling water for 6 minutes. (Use a home canner or put a rack on the bottom of the pot to protect the jars.) Leave the jars in the hot water until needed. The screw bands should be washed and rinsed and the snap lids heated in hot water (180°F).

Cut the apricots in half and remove the pits. Crack open 4 pits and extract the kernels. (Save the rest of the pits for noyau ice cream or for flavoring crème anglaise.)

Bring the simple syrup back to a boil. Working in batches (to avoid overcrowding), add the apricot halves to the boiling syrup and blanch just until they start to soften, about 2 minutes. Remove the jars from the water. Pack the warm apricots into the jars cut-side down. Pour the hot syrup over the apricots to cover, leaving ½ inch of headspace below the rim of the jar. Finally, add ¼ teaspoon pure ascorbic acid to each jar.

Wipe the rims of the jars clean and cap with the lids and screw bands. Place the jars back in the hot water so that they will remain upright and covered by 1 to 2 inches of water, bring to a boil, and boil for 25 minutes. Let cool and store in a cool dark place for up to a year.

Mia's Vin d'Orange

MAKES ABOUT 5 QUARTS

This invigorating but light apéritif was made popular at Chez Panisse by a pastry chef named Mia, who started making it at home in nearly commercial quantities to meet the demand from her colleagues.

8 Seville oranges

3 Meyer lemons or 2 sweet oranges

One 2-inch piece vanilla bean, split lengthwise

4½ liters (six 750 ml bottles) crisp white wine (such as Sauvignon Blanc)

¾ liter (3 cups) 80-proof vodka

1¾ cups sugar

Select citrus fruits that smell fragrant and floral when their skin is lightly scratched. Wash all the fruit and then slice into ½-inch-thick rounds. In a nonreactive container, combine the fruit, vanilla bean, wine, vodka, and sugar, stirring well to dissolve the sugar. Cover the container and store in a cool, dark place (or in the refrigerator) for 1 month. Once a week, stir and taste the mixture: If it seems too bitter, adjust by adding sugar; if it seems too sweet, add more fruit or wine.

After 1 month, strain and discard the solids and let the apéritif sit uncovered and undisturbed for a couple of days to allow the impurities to settle to the bottom. Carefully strain the liquid through several layers of cheesecloth, but stop pouring when you get to the cloudy part at the bottom. This process can be repeated until the vin d'orange is clear, though there is no harm in a bit of cloudiness.

Bottle the vin d'orange in clean wine bottles and cork tightly. It will keep for several months at cellar temperature, and longer if refrigerated.

VARIATION

~ Use 2 white grapefruit and 4 Ruby Red grapefruit instead of Seville oranges to make "vin de pamplemousse."

Vin de Pêche

MAKES ABOUT 6 CUPS

Nothing is as seductive as the bitter-almond perfume of fresh peach leaves, so delicate and so heady at the same time. Many years ago, when my friend Samantha was a Chez Panisse pastry chef, she planted a peach tree in her backyard to ensure a supply of tender leaves for our kitchens. Even though our coastal climate guarantees that the tree never yields much fruit, every year Samantha uses its young leaves for this delectable apéritif. My refrigerator never lacks a bottle.

120 fresh peach leaves, picked in late spring or early summer, washed and dried

One 750 ml bottle red wine (preferably a light, fruity Zinfandel)

½ cup Cognac

2 cups sugar

In a nonreactive container, combine all the ingredients and cover tightly. Store in a cool, dark place or in the refrigerator. After 1 month, strain the liquid (discarding the leaves) and pour into clean wine bottles. Cork tightly and serve well chilled over ice as an apéritif.

VARIATION

⤳ Use white wine instead of red, if you prefer, for an especially summery, lighter version.

Vanilla Extract

You can make homemade vanilla extract from whole vanilla beans and any strong alcohol. I've tried vodka and bourbon, too, but I prefer mild-flavored white rum, which is less overpowering.

Split 8 vanilla beans lengthwise, leaving ½ inch on each end intact. Scrape the pulp into a glass bottle or jar and add the split vanilla beans. Add 1½ cups mild-flavored white rum and cover the jar tightly. Let sit in a dark place for 6 to 8 weeks, or until the extract has a strong vanilla flavor. The flavor will continue to evolve. As the extract is used, more liquor can be added to keep the beans submerged; just let sit until the desired flavor returns. When mildly flavored, use it as a subtle addition to custards, ice creams, poached fruit syrups, drinks, and the like. If strongly flavored, use as you would any store-bought vanilla extract.

Lovage Syrup

MAKES ABOUT 1½ CUPS

Lovage is a perennial herb that looks like giant parsley but has a flavor more like celery. When it's plentiful in my garden, I sometimes add a handful of its chopped leaves to ground lamb or beef for hamburgers, but much of my harvest ends up in this unusual syrup. It has a beautiful bright green color and tastes like angelica, fennel, and celery—a perfect addition to a glass of Prosecco or Champagne for a refreshing and savory apéritif.

1 cup sugar   *1 cup lovage leaves*

Put the sugar and 1 cup water in a small saucepan. Cook over medium heat until the sugar has just dissolved. Pour the warm syrup into the jar of a blender. Add the lovage leaves, cover, and blend slowly and carefully, so as not to spray any hot liquid. Once the leaves are roughly puréed, increase the speed for about 10 seconds until the syrup is very smooth. Pour through a fine-mesh sieve, transfer to a clean bottle, and store in the refrigerator, where it will keep for 4 weeks.

To make a lovage spritzer: Fill an 8-ounce glass with ice, drizzle with 1 tablespoon of the lovage syrup, top off with sparkling water, and garnish with a squeeze of lemon.

VARIATION

꒱ Simple syrups can be infused with many flavors. Experiment with other fragrant herbs such as anise hyssop, lemon verbena, and various varieties of basil and mint.

Books

This is a short list of some of the books, old and new, that have exerted a powerful influence on my evolving pantry—and on the ingredients, homemade and otherwise, with which it's stocked.

The Art of Fermentation: An In-Depth Exploration of Essential Concepts and Processes from Around the World, by Sandor Ellix Katz

Artisan Cheese Making at Home: Techniques and Recipes for Mastering World-Class Cheeses, by Mary Karlin

Better Than Store-Bought: A Cookbook, by Helen Witty and Elizabeth Schneider Colchie

Cooking by Hand, by Paul Bertolli

Cowgirl Creamery Cooks, by Sue Conley and Peggy Smith

The Fannie Farmer Cookbook, by Marion Cunningham

Fermented Vegetables: Creative Recipes for Fermenting 64 Vegetables and Herbs in Krauts, Kimchis, Brined Pickles, Chutneys, Relishes, and Pastes, by Kirsten K. Shockey and Christopher Shockey

Fine Preserving: M. F. K. Fisher's Annotated Edition of Catherine Plagemann's Cookbook, by M. F. K. Fisher and Catherine Plagemann

Fish Forever: The Definitive Guide to Understanding, Selecting, and Preparing Healthy, Delicious, and Environmentally Sustainable Seafood, by Paul Johnson

Flatbreads and Flavors: A Baker's Atlas, by Jeffrey Alford and Naomi Duguid

French Roots: Two Cooks, Two Countries, and the Beautiful Food Along the Way, by Jean-Pierre Moullé and Denise Lurton Moullé

Honey from a Weed, by Patience Gray

My Bombay Kitchen: Traditional and Modern Parsi Home Cooking, by Niloufer Ichaporia King

The New Vegetarian Cooking for Everyone, by Deborah Madison

Nourishing Traditions: The Cookbook That Challenges Politically Correct Nutrition and the Diet Dictocrats, by Sally Fallon with Mary G. Enid, Ph.D.

On Food and Cooking: The Science and Lore of the Kitchen, by Harold McGee

One Good Dish, by David Tanis

Saving the Season: A Cook's Guide to Home Canning, Pickling, and Preserving, by Kevin West

Simple French Food, by Richard Olney

Tart and Sweet: 101 Canning and Pickling Recipes for the Modern Kitchen, by Kelly Geary and Jessie Knadler

The Tortilla Book, by Diana Kennedy

Twelve Recipes, by Cal Peternell

Acknowledgments

First and foremost, I would like to thank my daughter, Fanny, who helped write this book, and whose lovely ink illustrations bring my pantry to life in these pages. I could not have undertaken this book project without Samantha Greenwood, my right arm, who worked with me to develop the recipes alongside two wonderful former Chez Panisse cooks, Dana Berge and Jessica Washburn. I would like to thank Patty Curtan and Kelsie Kerr, two of my oldest friends and longtime collaborators, whose hard work on both volumes of *The Art of Simple Food* laid the foundation for this book and whose encouragement catalyzed its writing. This book would likewise not have been possible without the finesse of my dear friend Fritz Streiff. I also owe a debt of gratitude to my very patient editor, Pam Krauss. Finally, I would like to thank Martine Labro, Lindsey Shere, and Mary Jo Thoresen, who continue to inspire me with their commitment to economy, preservation, and beauty—and who have given me the most beautiful jars of plum jam, Meyer lemon marmalade, and crab apple jelly.

Index

© ERIC WOLFINGER

Fanny Singer is an art historian, curator, and illustrator based in London and Cornwall. Her mother, **Alice Waters**, the food activist and author, is chef and owner of Chez Panisse Restaurant in Berkeley, California, and the founder of the Edible Schoolyard Project.